Political, Economic, and Social Factors Affecting the Development of Russian Statehood:

Emerging Research and Opportunities

Bogdan Ershov
Voronezh State Technical University, Russia

Natalia Muhina
Voronezh State Technical University, Russia

Igor Ashmarov
Voronezh State Institute of Arts, Russia

A volume in the Advances in Public Policy and Administration (APPA) Book Series

IGI Global
DISSEMINATOR OF KNOWLEDGE

Published in the United States of America by
IGI Global
Information Science Reference (an imprint of IGI Global)
701 E. Chocolate Avenue
Hershey PA, USA 17033
Tel: 717-533-8845
Fax: 717-533-8661
E-mail: cust@igi-global.com
Web site: http://www.igi-global.com

Library of Congress Cataloging-in-Publication Data

Names: Ershov, Bogdan, 1982- author. | Muhina, Natalia, 1982- author. | Ashmarov, Igor, 1975- author.
Title: Political, economic, and social factors affecting the development of Russian statehood : emerging research and opportunities / by Bogdan Ershov, Natalia Muhina, and Igor Ashmarov.
Description: Hershey, PA : Information Science Reference, [2020]
Identifiers: LCCN 2019014117 | ISBN 9781522599852 (hc) | ISBN 9781522599883 (sc) | ISBN 9781522599869 (ebk)
Subjects: LCSH: Political culture--Russia (Federation). | Russia (Federation)--Politics and government--21st century. | Public institutions--Russia (Federation).
Classification: LCC DK510.763 .E77 2020 | DDC 947.086--dc23
LC record available at https://lccn.loc.gov/2019014117

This book is published in the IGI Global book series Advances in Public Policy and Administration (APPA) (ISSN: 2475-6644; eISSN: 2475-6652)

British Cataloguing in Publication Data
A Cataloguing in Publication record for this book is available from the British Library.

All work contributed to this book is new, previously-unpublished material.
The views expressed in this book are those of the authors, but not necessarily of the publisher.

For electronic access to this publication, please contact: eresources@igi-global.com.

Advances in Public Policy and Administration (APPA) Book Series

ISSN:2475-6644
EISSN:2475-6652

MISSION

Proper management of the public sphere is necessary in order to maintain order in modern society. Research developments in the field of public policy and administration can assist in uncovering the latest tools, practices, and methodologies for governing societies around the world.

The **Advances in Public Policy and Administration (APPA) Book Series** aims to publish scholarly publications focused on topics pertaining to the governance of the public domain. APPA's focus on timely topics relating to government, public funding, politics, public safety, policy, and law enforcement is particularly relevant to academicians, government officials, and upper-level students seeking the most up-to-date research in their field.

COVERAGE

- Government
- Law Enforcement
- Political Economy
- Politics
- Public Administration
- Public Funding
- Public Policy
- Resource Allocation
- Urban Planning

IGI Global is currently accepting manuscripts for publication within this series. To submit a proposal for a volume in this series, please contact our Acquisition Editors at Acquisitions@igi-global.com or visit: http://www.igi-global.com/publish/.

The Advances in Public Policy and Administration (APPA) Book Series (ISSN 2475-6644) is published by IGI Global, 701 E. Chocolate Avenue, Hershey, PA 17033-1240, USA, www.igi-global.com. This series is composed of titles available for purchase individually; each title is edited to be contextually exclusive from any other title within the series. For pricing and ordering information please visit http://www.igi-global.com/book-series/advances-public-policy-administration/97862. Postmaster: Send all address changes to above address.

Titles in this Series

For a list of additional titles in this series, please visit:
http://www.igi-global.com/book-series/advances-public-policy-administration/97862

Information Systems Strategic Planning for Public Service Delivery in the igital Era
Emanuel Camilleri (University of Malta, Malta)
Information Science Reference • ©2019 • 435pp • H/C (ISBN: 9781522596479) • US $225.00

Impacts of Political Instability on Economics in the MENA Region
Philippe W. Zgheib (Lebanese American University, Lebanon)
Information Science Reference • ©2019 • 300pp • H/C (ISBN: 9781522582472) • US $195.00

Social Partnership and Governance Under Crises
Carol Nelson (University of the West Indies, Jamaica)
Information Science Reference • ©2019 • 276pp • H/C (ISBN: 9781522589617) • US $185.00

Promoting Productive Cooperation Between Space Lawyers and Engineers
Anja Nakarada Pecujlic (University of Cologne, Germany) and Matteo Tugnoli (European Space Policy Institute, Austria)
Information Science Reference • ©2019 • 339pp • H/C (ISBN: 9781522572565) • US $215.00

Building a Sustainable Transportation Infrastructure for Long-Term Economic Growth
Olga V. Smirnova (East Carolina University, USA)
Engineering Science Reference • ©2019 • 309pp • H/C (ISBN: 9781522573968) • US $195.00

Industrial and Urban Growth Policies at the Sub-National, National, and Global Levels
Umar G. Benna (Benna Associates, Nigeria)
Information Science Reference • ©2019 • 418pp • H/C (ISBN: 9781522576259) • US $205.00

Analytics, Operations, and Strategic Decision Making in the Public Sector
Gerald William Evans (University of Louisville, USA) William E. Biles (University of Louisville, USA) and Ki-Hwan G. Bae (University of Louisville, USA)
Information Science Reference • ©2019 • 441pp • H/C (ISBN: 9781522575917) • US $215.00

For an entire list of titles in this series, please visit:
http://www.igi-global.com/book-series/advances-public-policy-administration/97862

IGI Global
DISSEMINATOR OF KNOWLEDGE

701 East Chocolate Avenue, Hershey, PA 17033, USA
Tel: 717-533-8845 x100 • Fax: 717-533-8661
E-Mail: cust@igi-global.com • www.igi-global.com

Table of Contents

Preface

AN OVERVIEW OF THE SUBJECT MATTER

The issue of Russian statehood has acquired exceptional relevance in recent years, round tables and large volumes of publications are devoted to it. Many modern politicians declare the strengthening of Russian statehood as one of the main strategic goals. At the same time, the general theoretical aspects of this subject are still not covered and not studied properly in Russian political science. The scope and content of the concept of "statehood" is still debatable. The elements of a political and legal theory that directly connect the phenomenon of statehood with the basic principles of the economic, regional, and foreign policy structure of the state, as well as the main components of its genesis, are also insufficiently developed. In the present work, an attempt is made to fill the indicated gaps and to provide our own version of the solution of this complex of scientific and practical problems.

It is important to note that in the entire history of Russia there have passed five main periods of state development: the Old Russian state, the Moscow state, the Russian Empire, the Soviet state and the Russian Federation. Research and study of these stages will help to trace the major milestones and the natural tendency of the state in Russia.

The beginning of the process of Russian statehood was laid in the Old Russian state, which arose in the middle of the ninth century with its center in Kiev and existed until the middle of the fifteenth century. The spiritual father and founder of the Old Russian state was destined to become Prince Vladimir Svyatoslavovich, called the Red Sun. Under him in 988, Russia adopted Orthodoxy as the state religion. This period was marked by the approval of the basic principles of statehood in Russia, the merging of its northern and southern centers, and the growth of the military-political and international influence of the state. As well as the onset of the stage of its fragmentation and the loss of centralized control, which is natural for the early feudal monarchies. The rise of the Moscow principality, which was the center of the "gathering of Russian lands", began in the fourteenth century in the Vladimir-Suzdal land. However, it took almost another hundred years for Moscow to finally consolidate its role as the organizing and spiritual center of the emerging Russian state.

Muscovy existed from the middle of the fifteenth century to the end of the seventeenth century. In this era, the final liberation of the Russian lands from the Golden Horde took place, the process of "gathering lands" around Moscow was completed, the main state-political, socio-economic and cultural principles of the Russian autocracy were formalized. After the wedding of Ivan IV to the kingdom in 1547, the most important reforms of state bodies, the judicial system, the army, the church followed. The formation of the Russian autocracy in the sixteenth century was accompanied by its success in the field of centralization of the state and the revitalization of foreign policy. The growth of international prestige of the Moscow state was also promoted by a significant expansion of its territory due to successful conquest campaigns and the colonization of new lands in the east. At the end of the XVI - the beginning of the XVII centuries, Russia entered a strip of deep state-political and socio-economic structural crisis, known as "Time of Troubles". Our country was on the verge of collapse and loss of its statehood. However, thanks to the patriotic rise, the crisis was overcome. The beginning of the reign of the newly elected Romanov dynasty on the Russian throne was marked by the restoration of the country's territorial integrity and the strengthening of its international prestige. During the seventeenth century, the main institutions of Russian absolutism were formed in the country, which created the prerequisites for the transformation of the Moscow kingdom into the Russian Empire.

The state of the Russian Empire covers the era from the end of the seventeenth century to the beginning of the twentieth century. During this time, the formation, flourishing and collapse of the Russian autocratic monarchy took place. The turning point in the formation of statehood in Russia was the reign of Peter I, whose reforms covered all spheres of state and public life, determining the development of our country for a long historical perspective. They were aimed at maximizing centralization in the management of the state, with its decisive influence on the life of all segments of society and the strict regulation of all its parties. After the death of Peter I, the Russian Empire entered the era of palace coups. During the period from 1725 to 1762, six autocrats were replaced on the Russian throne. The reign of Catherine II (1762-1796) was marked by the declared policy of "enlightened absolutism", an unprecedented increase in privileges as a noble class of the Russian Empire and at the same time an unprecedented scale of serfdom.

A DESCRIPTION OF THE TARGET AUDIENCE

It is important to note that the above information is based on the fruitful work of the renewed national historiography. At the same time, the authors sought to be receivers of the best, critically interpreting what was done by our and foreign historians of previous generations.

The research of these topics is based on the problem-chronological principle, which helps to understand the complex logic of the historical process.

The presented information has cognitive, intellectual, developmental and nurturing functions. Therefore, it will be useful for high school students, applicants, students, teachers, teachers of higher educational institutions, as well as all those who are interested in this issue.

Also, this work is aimed at providing assistance to students studying special courses of political science content. It is designed to facilitate the development of the necessary theoretical minimum required to understand the history and current state of Russian statehood. Thus, the task is set to help students in detail and substantively get acquainted with each of the above listed components of the life activity of the Russian state. The information presented in the respective chapters will not only have a cognitive political value, but will also prove useful in studying related disciplines of the corresponding profile.

In a number of cases, not only issues facing the state and society are described, but also options for their possible solution are proposed. Of course, many of them are not indisputable, but voicing them can give students an impulse to further understand these problems.

This work will be useful in the methodological purposes of teaching courses related to the problems of domestic statehood, and will contribute to the solution of urgent and extremely important issues.

According to the authors, the information presented should contribute to the moral development of the individual, the formation of citizenship and patriotism, the preservation and consolidation of human value orientations, help develop independent creative thinking, motives, skills and abilities to act for the benefit of society.

Despite various forecasts regarding the development of Russian society and the country as a whole, it is important that the state bears the main responsibility for reforming society and carrying out all activities related to the creation of a new lifestyle and the emergence of a state mechanism. And this, in turn, dictates the need for a deep analysis of the relationship between the state and society, the functional characteristics of the state, which will reveal the degree of change in its activities, goals and objectives during the transition to a market economy, to a new social order.

It is also important to trace how relations between the state and property develop, that is, the key, fundamental relations that determine the type of statehood at a certain stage of its development.

The prospects for the development of multinational statehood cannot be assessed without taking into account the national factor, including historical, socio-cultural and other differences between the peoples inhabiting the country. The role of the modern state structure of Russia in the implementation of two interrelated tasks is the preservation of the territorial integrity of the Russian Federation and at the same time strengthening the status of its subjects.

Equally important are state-confessional relations that impose a special imprint on the value system of a particular statehood and dictate the need for a deep and comprehensive understanding of the relationship between church and state.

It is impossible to assess statehood from the point of view of its progressiveness, legal orientation without taking into account the interrelations of the individual and the state, the individual and society, the state of affairs with respect for human rights, their guarantee and real possibilities to use these rights. Human rights and freedoms have become the highest value of modern society and a priority interest, more significant than welfare and material security. They acquired tremendous importance in the face of increasing interstate integration ties and the desire to build a rule-of-law state in our country.

The realities of modern statehood provide the basis for precisely such an approach to the analysis of modern Russian statehood in order to identify legally significant trends and patterns of its development.

A DESCRIPTION OF THE IMPORTANCE OF EACH OF THE CHAPTER SUBMISSIONS

Chapter 1. The state-legal development of Russian society is characterized by general laws that are characteristic of any society. But it has features characteristic only for Russia. Hence the imperative need to study such uniqueness in order to establish the causes and factors affecting the life processes of Russian society, to form an attitude towards new values and ideals arising during the transition to a new social system.

Chapter 2. During the eighteenth and early twentieth centuries, the Russian state carried out modernization of higher and local governments, as well as many other aspects of society. According to the form of government, Russia became an absolute monarchy and a unitary state, which, however, granted certain autonomy to a number of national margins of the Empire.

Chapters 3-5. An attempt to create a monarchy at the beginning of the 20th century failed because of the conservatism of the ruling circles and the radical sentiments of the politically active part of the population (mostly citizens). The formation and activity of Soviet statehood was based on the rejection of the theory of separation of powers, civil society and the rule of law. Formally, being a parliamentary republic, in fact, the USSR had a completely different system of power and decision-making. The collapse of the USSR and the formation of the modern Russian state led to the transformation of the corresponding elements. In general, the Russian Federation is a segmental type of state form, since many characteristics of such a model correspond to the real state of affairs. According to the form of government, Russia is a presidential republic, despite the constitutional consolidation of certain features of a mixed (presidential-parliamentary) republic.

The study of domestic historical experience, awareness of the possibility of its use can expand the problematic sphere of modern public research, help identify the best approaches to the reform of the institutions of the Russian statehood. It should be noted that modern Russian society is in dire need of an effective system of public administration, much is being done in this area, and at the same time there is practically no special body professionally dealing with this very complex issue that does not recognize amateurish approaches. It is not by chance that even in countries with a well-established state system, for decades there have been relevant special departments - administrative reform committees, the ministries of the civil service and public administration, a commission to study the effectiveness of the civil service and public administration.

The main task of the beginning of the reform of the Russian statehood was the institutional consolidation of the transition from the Soviet type of government to the model of the rule of law state. To date, certain successes have been achieved in this area: 1) the Constitution of the Russian Federation and the constitutions (charters) of its subjects have been adopted in accordance with the principles of the rule of law; 2) a system of state bodies more or less corresponding to the model of the legal state has been formed; 3) the fundamental federal law was adopted and the process of the formation of local self-government began, etc.

Chapters 6-8. Now the reform of Russian statehood has come close to its new stage. Its main task is to implement the model of the legal state in practice, through the functional development and normative consolidation of new forms and methods of work characteristic of the state governing bodies of the legal state.

Administrative reform, about which President of the Russian Federation V.V. Putin stated in his message, is beginning to gain momentum. The plan of administrative reform proposed by the Cabinet has been approved. It seems that the current stage of the reform implies a change in the structures of federal executive bodies. Summarizing the above, I would like to draw attention to the fact that it is the provision of quality services to the population in the economic, legal, socio-cultural and other areas that is the main criterion for the effectiveness of public administration. And perhaps more than ever in a timely manner, it is not the state, but the society, that is to start reforming. It is rightly said that the most valuable resource now is not land, not technology, but man. In other words - the system of organizing the work of people.

The cultural policy of the state is one of the priorities of national development, and lies at the heart of the socio-economic and political spheres of life of any country in the world, including in Russia.

According to official data, there are about 146.5 million people in modern Russia. Therefore, it is extremely important to study the processes occurring in the modern Russian multinational environment. The future of the country depends on how the problems of its population are solved, including in the sphere of culture and art. The same is true for Russia.

The state cultural policy determines the main strategic line of the state to ensure the socio-economic, political and cultural development of Russia in order to foster a sense of patriotism and respect for the history and culture of their Fatherland, other peoples and respect for human rights. The state cultural policy must be honest and responsible to its people so that the people can trust their ruler and their state.

State policy in the field of culture is an effective tool for making changes and adjustments in the relevant field from the position of the governing political authorities of a particular country. Since the culture of any country is a collective intelligence, therefore, government policy deals with its regulation and modification, and at the same time, government policy itself is under the great influence of this collective intelligence.

Without such changes and adjustments, the situation can quickly change, and not in the best direction for the country, so we have to state that it is much better for the country when there is such a targeted state policy in the country. It all starts with setting goals and objectives, developing development plans and programs, including culture, therefore, state planning and programming in the field of culture and art: in theatre, cinema, circus, etc. It starts with the first management function, namely planning. At the same time, other management functions, including organization, motivation and control, cannot be avoided either. State policy in a particular sphere, the sphere of culture, art, science, education, health care, etc., in its deep essence, is management, including management in the sphere of culture and art.

Obviously, one thing is that without financial support from the state, the sphere of culture and art, even if it can be commercialized, will not be able to effectively develop as it does with the support of the state and its institutions, especially in Russia. The absolute majority of institutions of culture and art, education and science, and health care in Russia are either state or municipal, which in Russian conditions is almost the same.

The state policy in the field of culture in Russia and in the USSR in the XX century has chronologically at least three evolutionary independent periods.

Firstly, it is the culture of the Russian empire at the beginning of the 20th century, before the 1917 revolution. Secondly, it is the Soviet culture, or the culture of the USSR, from the moment of its formation in 1922 until its collapse in 1991. Thirdly, it is the culture of modern Russia, the Russian Federation, starting in January 1992 and ending in XX century, although this culture continues to develop successfully in the present, continuing this third stage of its development.

The urgency of the problems of formation and implementation of state policy is also associated with the identification of priority areas and new criteria for its performance that would meet today's requirements. Questions of the history of state policy in the USSR are directly related to modernity.

The main task of the state should be to create a favourable socio-economic and spiritual-moral environment for using young energy in the life of the country and mechanisms for its support, social initiatives, helping young people in identifying and realizing their hobbies, needs, life prospects through a well-thought-out, scientifically based state politicians.

Attitude to the sphere of culture has always been related to the state and society. Culture and art are the most active components of civil society. State cultural policy is usually aimed at ensuring the continuity of generations, the preservation and development of national culture, the education of young people, etc. Therefore, a competent and qualified cultural policy will always be a priority for any state.

State policy in Russia brings a culture sanctified by the government to the masses of the country's population, to the masses of young people; it has a selective spiritual and moral basis and pursues strict educational goals. General policy institutions, secondary schools, colleges, colleges, technical schools, institutes and universities, as well as specially created youth organizations that meet in their spirit the requirements imposed by the top leadership of the country and the state in Russia act as a conductor of state policy.

State policy in Russia allows for the necessary control by the state and shaping the mentality of the population, especially young people, as well as their ideas, attitudes and mindsets in accordance with the goals and objectives of the country's political leadership, to keep it within the necessary institutional frameworks and borders.

CONCLUSION

At the beginning of the 21st century, according to the United Nations assessment in the world ranking, Russia occupied 62-68 places in the Human Development Index. Among the most important indicators of the rating: life expectancy, the level of real incomes of the population, the quality and availability of education. Objective analysis reveals the unnatural nature of this situation, since in terms of the level of natural wealth and many other parameters, Russia ranks first among the countries of the world; the achievements of past periods testify to the greatness and great potential of the people. But there was a transformation of state priorities, at the low level the most important state functions in the field of education were performed. Investing in the future - in humans should certainly become priorities of the state budget policy, because general education is one of the decisive conditions for Russia's competitiveness in the world. The direction of investment is the formation in the educational sphere of social institutions that would create opportunities for the most effective implementation of budgetary funds, public funds and business to achieve the goals of state educational policy.

Objects of long-term modernization in general education include the academic subject area, the social organization of an educational institution, and the school sociocultural environment. Russian statehood has typological features that correspond to the ethnocultural uniqueness of Russia. Consideration of the Russian statehood in its many connections, aspects, functions, etc., makes it possible to form a holistic view of Russian reality from a wider perspective.

Each state has a special type of spiritual and material organization, a particular mentality of the people, the peculiarity of the economic structure, and other features. Based on this provision, it can be concluded that, in Russia, not all democratic institutions will be viable, but only those that correspond to the way of life of Russian society, correspond to the domestic political and legal culture. As the experience of many countries, including Russia, shows, insufficient consideration of value orientations and the state of culture can doom reform to failure, lead to a dead-end path of development. Without an appropriate cultural type of people, it is impossible to establish in the country an optimal state system ensuring the safety of citizens and rights, effective management in the interests of the people.

Orthodoxy had an impact on the development of Russian statehood, as it had a decisive influence on the popular mentality, as evidenced by the cultural differences between the Slavs who profess the Orthodox faith and Catholicism. Being basically an ideological phenomenon, Orthodoxy gave a conciliar understanding of human nature.

The ideology of society has always been based on traditional Orthodox ideals, imbued with conciliar values, proclaiming equality, communal personal relations. This fact contributed to the perception by society of the ideology of Bolshevism.

The function of ideology should be to define the goals and objectives of the development of the state. At the same time, ideology should be based on spiritual and moral values corresponding to cultural traditions, formed by history and Orthodoxy as a tradition.

When considering the socio-cultural specifics of the Russian state, we can draw the following conclusions. For the optimal functioning of the state, the political and economic elites should take into account the needs of the mass strata of society, foresee their reactions to the reform processes taking place in life.

The ideas of paternalism in modern Russia are still strong and are likely to be strong in the long term.

Acknowledgment

The authors of this book express deep gratitude to Ms. Josie Dadeboe, Assistant Development Editor IGI Global, and Ms. Jan Travers, Director of Intellectual Property and Contracts IGI Global, in editing and publishing book.

Introduction

The monograph presented to the reader is a summary of the main chronological stages in the development of the history of Russia, from early times to the present day (late 20th century).

The sequence of presentation of the material on the sections and topics indicated in the monograph corresponds to the concepts of Russian history generally accepted in Russian historical science. At the end of the monograph is a traditional bibliography list and acknowledgment.

Chapter 1
Factors of Political Development of Russia From the 10th to the 18th Centuries

Bogdan Ershov
Voronezh State Technical University, Russia

Natalia Muhina
Voronezh State Technical University, Russia

ABSTRACT

The chapter deals with the formation and development of Russian statehood from the 10th to the 18th centuries. It was at this time that domestic statehood was formed in very peculiar conditions. The following factors greatly influenced the specifics of Russian statehood: peasant, national, geopolitical, modernization. Throughout its history, Russia has gone through five major periods of state development: the Old Russian state, Muscovy, the Russian Empire, the Soviet state, and the Russian Federation. The process of Russian statehood was birthed in the ancient Russian state, which arose in the middle of the 9th century with its center in Kiev and existed until the middle of the 15th century. This period was marked by the approval of the basic principles of statehood in Russia, the merging of its northern and southern centers, and the growth of the military-political and international influence of the state.

DOI: 10.4018/978-1-5225-9985-2.ch001

INTRODUCTION

For more than a millennium, there has been Russian statehood. Her story is a matter of pride and admiration. Previous generations of Russians at the cost of enormous losses and deprivations created one of the most powerful powers on earth, defended its freedom and independence.

Russian statehood is the emergence and development of the Russian state, its various types, forms and functions at various stages of Russian history, the continuity and renewal of the political, structural and territorial organization of Russian society, i.e. state-legal processes occurring over a long period of life of the Russian ethnic group.

The formation and development of Russian statehood has taken a number of centuries. At the same time, domestic statehood was formed in very peculiar conditions. The following factors had a great influence on the specifics of modern Russian statehood: peasant, national, geopolitical, modernization issues.

Throughout its history, Russia has gone through five major periods of state development: the Old Russian state, Muscovy, the Russian Empire, the Soviet state, and the Russian Federation.

THE BEGINNING OF THE FORMATION OF THE RUSSIAN STATE

The process of Russian statehood began in the Old Russian state, which arose in the middle of the 9th century with its center in Kiev and existed until the middle of the 15th century. The spiritual father and founder of the Old Russian state was destined to become Prince Vladimir Svyatoslavovich, called the Red Sun. Under him in 988, Russia adopted Orthodoxy as the state religion. This period was marked by the approval of the basic principles of statehood in Russia, the merging of its northern and southern centers, and the growth of the military-political and international influence of the state.

With the advent of Yaroslav Vladimirovich (the Wise) to power in 1019, the state reached a high level of development. This was facilitated by the victory over the Pechenegs, which was gained in 1036, and the far-sighted policy, during which the first set of laws "Russkaya Pravda" appeared, the church reform took place, and the main forces were directed to the establishment of trade relations.

The sons of Yaroslav, having failed to resolve the issue of inheriting power after his death, plunged the country into a state of fragmentation for a long time, aggravated by the invasion of the Polovtsian menace. In 1068, the brothers suffered their first defeat in the war with the nomads, soon after which an uprising broke out in Kiev.

The problem of internecine conflicts was briefly resolved with the advent of Vladimir Monomakh in 1113. The talented ruler managed to suppress numerous rebellions and to win a number of victories over the Polovtsy. Much was done to consolidate the power of the prince and alleviate the heavy burden of the peasants. The course adopted by Vladimir Monomakh was continued under the rule of his son Mstislav the Great. The successful, but short-lived rule of Mstislav Vladimirovich ended in 1132, after which the country was again divided into principalities (Ershov, 2017).

This decay occurred under the influence of the feudal mode of production. The external defense of the Russian land was especially weak. The princes of individual principalities carried out their separate policies, taking into account primarily the interests of the local feudal nobility and entered into endless internecine wars. This led to the loss of centralized control and to a strong weakening of the state as a whole. Vladimir-Suzdal principality, later the dominant territory of North-Eastern Russia, covered the area between the Oka and Volga. On its territory lay the path from White Lake along Shezhne to the Volga. The principality was connected not only with the Novgorod trade, which already meant a lot, but also with the European trade, and along the Volga with the Caspian Sea, Central Asia, the Celestial Empire, and Byzantium. Along the Moscow River led the way to Kolomna, along the Oka to the Volga and along the Klyazma to the Volga. Vladimir principality was part of the once powerful and united, but in the XIII century Kiev principality snapped up into pieces. Pereyaslavl became an independent principality. Principality: Chernigov, Novgorod-Seversk, Galitsko-Volynsk, Smolensk - became independent. The former Kievan Rus was cut into two parts: the South and the Northeast. The center of South Russia due to the loss of its political significance by Kiev was the Galician principality headed by Yaroslav Osmomysl. In the Northeast part, Vladimir-Suzdal land became dominant. Along with Galich, another political center was formed - Vladimir, which was protected by impassable forests, swamps, rivers, and the Ryazan-Murom principality.

In 1147 appears the first mention of Moscow, associated with the name of Yuri Dolgoruky. Twice this prince tried to seize the throne of Kiev and become the sole ruler, but in both cases he failed to gain a foothold in this field for a long time. For a short time, Yury Dolgoruky's son, Andrey Bogolyubsky, managed to halt the disintegration process. At the same time, the prince's immediate patrimony, the Vladimir – Suzdal principality, received great strength and significant development.

Since 1173, the princely throne has been occupied by another son of Vladimir Monomakh - Vsevolod the Big Nest. During the years of rule, this prince undertook several successful military campaigns, tried to unite the Russian lands around Vladimir, strengthened trade relations and strengthened the economy.

The weakening of Russia by internal disputes led to the fact that in 1237 the ruinous procession of the Golden Horde began on the Russian lands. Under the rule of the Tatar-Mongol yoke were almost all Russian cities. For many years they were forced to pay tribute and were regularly subjected to punitive raids, which very soon led to an economic recession and a weakening of Russia's position at the international level.

At the same time, along and following the march of Batu, the western neighbors (Lithuania, the Crusaders) of Rus made several attempts to seize the Russian lands adjacent to their possessions.

1239 - the campaign of Yaroslav Vsevolodovich near Smolensk to expel the Lithuanian regiments who came to fight on the Russian land.

Summer of 1240 - the Crusaders marched on Pskov and Novgorod, followed by the German knights.

Swedish crusader ships appeared on the Neva at the same time as Baty's forces were under Kiev. At this time, since 1236 Alexander, the son of Yaroslav, the grandson of Vsevolod, reigned in Novgorod. In the days of the invasion of Batu, he was preparing for the defense of Novgorod. Having learned about the invasion of the Swedes, he began to wait for them, hurrying to meet them on the Neva. July 15 in the battle on the Neva Jari Birger suffered a crushing defeat. Alexandra named Nevsky. As soon as the Swedes fought off, the knights of the Teutonic Order appeared, they defeated the Pskov regiments and approached Pskov, burnt the suburbs and besieged the city. Then the knights built a fortress in Kopor'e, imposed a tribute in the conquered volosts.

In 1241, the Mongol-Tatars entered Europe: Hungary, Poland, Moravia, Lower Silesia. At this time, Alexander at the head of the Nizhny Novgorod squad fought with the German invaders. Pskov did not beat off, but Koporye was cleared of Germans. After such actions of the eastern and western neighbors of Russia and the Grand Duke of Vladimir Yaroslav, the question arose: how to fight on all sides. Analyzing the military-political situation of that time, Yaroslav had to choose the path of further development of Russia. Properly assessing the situation, Yaroslav, and then Alexander Nevsky, decided to secure, first of all, his eastern borders, then to turn his gaze against the Crusaders and the Lithuanian princes. This step did not reflect the mood of the people, whose patriotism was always very strong, but brought stability to the Russian land, but it was time for a respite. A huge influence in this period acquired the figure of Alexander Nevsky. Baty, seeing the deterioration of the political conjuncture on the western borders of the Novgorod and Pskov lands, once again installed Alexander Yaroslavich in Novgorod, capable of stopping the movement of the Crusaders. After a trip to the Horde in 1242, Alexander assembled the Novgorod regiments, and calmly moved behind his rear toward Pskov, expelled the crusaders from there, and entered the Peipsi Land, into the possession of the Order. There, on Lake Peipsi, one of the greatest battles of the Middle Ages unfolded, in which Alexander's talent as a commander manifested itself brilliantly. The battle took place on April 5 and received in the history the name of the Battle of the Ice. German knights lined up a wedge, or rather, a narrow and very deep column, whose task was reduced to a massive strike at the center of the Novgorod army. The Russian army was built according to the classical scheme developed by Svyatoslav. The center is a foot regiment with archers advanced, and on the flanks is cavalry. The Novgorod chronicle and the German chronicle unanimously assert that the wedge broke through the Russian center, but at that time the Russian cavalry struck the flanks, and the knights were surrounded. In a stubborn battle, the Russians broke the knights. Order lost 500 knights, captured more than 50.

The victory on Lake Peipsi raised the prestige of Alexander very highly and at the same time strengthened the political influence of his father, Prince Yaroslav of Vladimir. It should be noted here that immediately after the invasions of Batu in Northeastern and Southern Russia, the decisive word in political life belonged to the Horde khans, since any disobedience was like death. Batu immediately reacted to the strengthening of the house of Yaroslav. He called him to the Horde with his son. Establishing a connection, to some extent similar to vassalit, allowed us to do the restoration of the ruined and preserve the beginnings of the statehood of Russia.

However, the reign of Grand Duke Alexander Nevsky ended as a result of his unexpected death in 1263.

In the history of the Russian land, a new stage began, marked not only by the long confrontation of the Moscow and Tver princedoms, but also by the emergence of their confrontation on the all-Russian political arena. At this time, in the political tactics of the Volga Horde, a new technique emerged, which consisted in the use of confrontation between large states, in our case between the Vladimir and Lithuanian-Russian principalities. The political influence of the Horde began to manifest itself in the constant changing and setting the princes at each other, the constant strengthening of the weak and the weakening of the strong. The economy of Northern Russia, destroyed even during the time of Batu, was going through a process of a long formation, weighted to the same time by constant requisitions in the form of tribute and just predatory raids. But, nevertheless, Russia gained political and military forces in the 60-70s and was preparing for a fight with the Horde, which still retained its political and military potential (Gorinov, 1995).

With the beginning of the rule of Daniel, the son of Alexander Nevsky, the separation and strengthening of the Moscow principality began. Due to a better location of Moscow, compared to Kiev and Vladimir, it becomes a new center, around which the gradual unification of the Russian lands begins.

Grand Duke Ivan Danilovich, nicknamed by the people of Kalita, continued the unifying policy of his father. In 1327, the only uprising of the Russian people against the Horde yoke occurred. The time has come for Ivan Kalita. Having no choice, he had to lead the Tatar army to the then Moscow-based Tver, in order to avoid major raids by the Tatars. For this service in 1332, Ivan became the Grand Duke. Already from the time of Ivan, they began to collect surpluses from tribute, and to preserve, however, they did not quite know what to do with them. During the reign of Ivan Kalita acquired international political weight and began to lay claim to the entire ancient Russian heritage of the Lithuanian-Russian principality, which united Smolensk, Podolsk, Vitebsk, Minsk, Lithuania, and subsequently the Middle Dnieper region. The Horde encouraged and incited more contradictions between the two great principalities, alternately taking the side of one of the parties, following the policy developed by Genghis Khan. All these achievements of the Horde policy in Eastern Europe turned out to be possible, apparently because important changes took place in the Horde itself. At the beginning of the 14th century, the Juchi Ulus broke up into the Blue and White Hordes. Subsequently, the White Horde, located in the basin of the Volga and Don rivers, in the Crimea and in the North Caucasus, was given the name Golden Horde. Uzbek became the Khan of this Horde. Under his leadership, the Golden Horde intensified its oppression to the Russian lands, which contributed to the territorial growth of

Lithuania and its prince Gedemin. To somehow equalize the two states, Ivan Kalita also received the patronage of the Horde. In 1321, Gedemin took Kiev, which turned his principality into both the southern and western centers of statehood. The period of feudal fragmentation ended in Poland, where Casimir the Great was crowned on April 25, 1332. In 1345 Olgerd became the prince of Lithuania, during whose life the Grand Duchy of Lithuania surpassed the territory of the Great Vladimir Principality. It should be noted that the Horde did not prevent the formation of such a powerful state as opposed to Vladimir and Moscow (Klyuchevsky, 1995).

At the end of the XIV century, Moscow occupied a dominant place among all other cities of North-Eastern Russia. Ivan Kalita did a great deal to strengthen Moscow and to ensure that the Horde Baskaks and gangs of Horde robbers no longer appeared in Russia. Outwardly, he expressed complete submission to the Horde Khan, but at the same time created the material prerequisites for the strengthening of Moscow and its elevation. Showing cunning, prudence and cruelty for a short time he was able to make Moscow the most developed and prosperous principality, to join Ryazan and Uglich. But, dying, except for the treasury and the principality, Kalita left an unresolved issue with Novgorod, a rivalry with the Lithuanian principality and the Horde yoke. Ivan Kalita died in March 1341 in the same year as Gedemin. After their death, new rulers appeared on the scene: Olgerd Gedeminovich and Simeon Ivanych Proud, both powerful and strong-willed.

Immediately after the death of Kalita, a dispute broke out over the reign in Vladimir, but the Horde, as opposed to Lithuania, was forced to leave the reign of a Moscow house headed by Simeon, who received the Great Vladimir principality. Simeon was able to muffle the incessant hostility with Tver and in 1346 he married the sister of Prince of Tver Vsevolod Aleksandrovich. Dangers lay in wait for the Moscow prince from the side of Lithuania and the Horde. It was dangerous to resolve the dispute with Lithuania because of the wrath of the Horde, while Simeon still had no strength to fight against the Horde. But the main problem Simeon was Novgorod. While the Horde controlled the political and economic life of Northeastern Russia, the capture of Novgorod was associated with a conflict with Lithuania, which believed that Novgorod was or should be part of the Great Lithuanian-Russian principality. Simeon nevertheless led Novgorod to obedience, approved the authority of the grand-ducal power on Novgorod land, but Moscow did not even try to achieve complete subordination of Novgorod. And he was right, since the excessive strengthening of Moscow at the expense of Novgorod would cause displeasure of the Horde.

Tver calmed down, the Horde got bogged down in the war with the Hulagids. There was silence on the Russian land. It would seem that fate had handed Simeon the sword of liberation. Perhaps the clash with the Horde would have happened much earlier than the Battle of Kulikovo, but a plague epidemic rolled in from Europe. Russia and Lithuania were weakened and depopulated. Simeon, who died during the epidemic, left a testament in which he "ordered us to live together." Moscow principality by inheritance from Simeon passed to his brother Ivan (Kornilov, 2004).

The chronicles did not particularly note the reign of Ivan Ivanovich - Russia healed the wounds inflicted by the plague. The chroniclers, relying, apparently, on popular rumor, called Ivan Prince Merciful, such nicknames are rarely given to rulers without foundation. Ivan ruled from 1353 to 1359, he hurried to secretly strengthen his principality, encouraging the resettlement of crafts and industry people closer to Moscow. It was under Ivan that the activities of Sergey Radonezhsky, one of the leaders of the Kulikovo victory, began.

Ivan died, leaving the principality to his son, Dmitry, who was 9 years old this year. By the XIV century, the proclamation of the Grand Duke of Vladimir depended on the will of the Khan. Rivals of the kind of Kalita and the Moscow princes sometimes divined the principles of the Horde policy and found that with the death of Ivan a favorable situation was created in order to wrest the great reign from the Moscow princes. The main rival of Dmitry can be considered Dmitry of Suzdal, for a long time competing with Dmitry Ivanovich, but in 1362 forced to flee from Vladimir. From 1362, you can start the countdown of the movement of Russia to the Kulikovo battle, this is the year when Dmitry Ivanovich was confirmed during the Great Reign and when chroniclers noticed Temnik Mamai in the Horde. No one then could have imagined that in the future they would face a clash - one of the largest in the history of the Middle Ages, that one would lead the liberation struggle of the Russian people, the other would come to the defense of the kingdom created by Batu. Dmitry sought to unite Northeastern Russia, Mamai - to stop feudal strife and to restore the power of the monarchy. The whole question was whether Dmitry Ivanovich would be able to unite around Moscow the lands of North-Eastern Russia and the Russian people before Mamai could mobilize the Horde forces to suppress the Moscow "sedition".

In 1367, Dmitri laid the Stone Kremlin in Moscow. Construction was carried out very quickly, stone walls grew in front of our eyes.

In 1371, Dmitry was only 20 years old. To prepare such an army that the Horde would consider him dangerous is not a matter of one day or one year. There is no doubt that in adolescence and in his youth, Dmitri was surrounded by wise counselors whom Simeon ordered to listen. One of Dmitriy's brilliant virtues was the ability to listen to advisers, to choose the necessary and useful, regardless of ambitious advisers.

By the 14th century, the strength of infantry, forgotten in the early Middle Ages, was fully appreciated in Europe. However, it's not just oblivion. Feudal lords in every way removed plebeians from participation in military affairs for fear that armed common people would rise against their power. The infantry was revived in the cities at the initiative of the city authorities and against the feudal lords.

The pre-Bolster period in the Russian military was in many ways reformative. In order to work out the tactics of fighting with the Horde, it was necessary, first of all, to know its tactics and weigh what to oppose to the military art of the Horde. The first tactical task is, of course, to repel a rifle strike. It was decided simply: against the shooters it is necessary to put the shooters.

However, after a small-arms strike, in the case of unabated resistance, the Horde switched to a frontal attack in the cavalry formation; therefore, it is necessary to prevent the equestrian battle and impose a foot on the Horde. Horse regiments acted here as guard flank, guard and reserve regiments. For practicing all tactical techniques, Dmitry needed time. Russia was preparing for the accomplishment of the Horde yoke, and this could not pass unnoticed in the Horde. In 1373, Mamai attacked Ryazan for reconnaissance purposes. September 1, 1375 was finally pacified Tver. In the winter of 1377, Dmitry Volynsky marched on Bulgar. Everything spoke for the fact that the decisive battle was near. In the winter of 1377-1378, Dmitry delivered a blow to the Mordovian princes, the allies of Mamaia. Favorably the situation in the Horde. Mamai had 2 strong competitors: Tokhtamysh and Tamerlan.

For Mamai and Dmitry, the time for responsible decisions had come, it was impossible to wait any longer. But Mamai still underestimated the forces of Moscow, otherwise he would have taken up the whole Horde, instead of first sending Begich and five more temniki, which were defeated on the Vosher river by the combined forces of North-Eastern Russia under the command of Dmitry Ivanovich. As soon as Mamai learned about Begich's defeat, he immediately gathered in a campaign all the forces that were at his disposal at that moment (Pavlenko, 2000).

On August 15, 1380, Dmitry appointed the gathering of all the regiments in Kolomna, as soon as it became clear that Mamai was planning his invasion for the end of the summer. Khan at this time broke the camp on the river Beautiful Sword.

In Kolomna, equipped the shelves. The chronicles say that the Russian land has not seen such a huge force for a long time. From Kolomna, the path of the united troops lay through the Oka and Lopasne, there beyond the borders of the Ryazan principality, Dmitri's ally, this was Dmitri's strategic plan. The Moscow army moved in complete silence, on August 30 the crossing over the Oka was completed, on September 6 the army approached the Don, where Dmitry planned to meet Mamai. The meeting place was chosen Kulikovo field, and not by chance. The entire geography of the Kulikovo field favored the Russian army: the river, forest and swampy flanks, the elevation in place of the camp of the Russian troops. Mamai was moving to the Kulikov Field with the Beautiful Swords. On the night of September 7–8, Russian troops crossed the Don River and entered battle formation in the watershed between Smolka and Nizhny Dubik. The left flank of the Russian troops, to which the Tatars 'main attack was supposed to fall, moved to the muddy shores of Smolka, a reserve and an ambush regiment were located behind the left flank. The right flank was protected by the marshy shores of Nepryadva, as well as heavily armed Pskov and Polotsk horse guards. In the center - a big rati, all city regiments were brought together. The advanced regiment was still part of a large regiment, but the task of the guard regiment was to set up a battle and return to service.

On the morning of September 8, a thick, impenetrable fog stood over the Kulikovo field, which dissipated only by twelve o'clock. On the Kulikovo Field, the Horde had superiority in cavalry and threatened the Russian flank. The horde sought to encircle the Russians and kill their ranks with a ram attack. The Russians took the fight in active defense. This was another tactical idea of Dmitry. After the Horde ram attack was repelled, and it dismounted, the Russian soldiers, in order to remove numerical superiority, undertook a complicated maneuver of the left flank: retreated, lured the right flank of the Horde into an ambush, destroyed it; and then the Russian troops surrounded the main forces of Mamai. The defeat of Mamaia, and the Horde troubles that followed, which led to the final disintegration of the predatory state, the demonstration of the superiority of Russian military art over the military art of the enemy, the strengthening of state power in Russia are noticeable consequences of the battle on the Kulikovo Field. At the same time, the Kulikovo battle marked the beginning of the revival of the national self-consciousness of the Russian people.

A huge role in this victory was played by Dmitry Donskoy. This is a historical figure who managed to understand the people's aspirations and unite all Russian people to accomplish them and reconcile the most acute social contradictions before the decisive clash with the oppressors. This is his merit in domestic politics. But he not only revived the best traditions of military art, he enriched him with new principles of strategy and tactics, in incredibly difficult conditions he managed to arm and train the army. Also, his companions in all his affairs were Metropolitan Alexei and hegumen of the Trinity Monastery Sergius of Radonezh. These people were able, under the auspices of the Russian church, to gather all the persecuted people under the single banner of liberation. The Kulikov victory created a qualitatively new political situation in Eastern Europe, in which artificially restrained unification processes were given room for their development. With the Kulikov victory began the steady ascent of Moscow, the capital of the Russian lands.

Now there were signs of increased personal influence of Dmitry Donskoy. Here I must say that Dmitry fought not only with Mamai, but also with the Lithuanian prince Yagailo, whose army during the Kulikovo battle stood with Dmitry almost behind his back, because Don don't have been able to fight with the combined army and therefore tricky maneuver cut off Yagailo from Mamai . In 1381, Tokhtamysh gives a label to the great reign of Jagaila. By putting Yagailo as a counterbalance to Moscow, Tokhtamysh decided to invade Northeastern Russia to thwart the plans of Dmitry and his Metropolitan Cyprian to create an all-Russian antiordynian front (Platonov, 2005).

Not feeling the strength to begin the invasion in the way Batu and Mamai did, Tokhtamysh attacked Russia sneaking, counting on surprise. Dmitry entrusted the defense of Moscow to Cyprian and Andrei Olgerdovich's son, Prince Ostey, leaving Princess Evdokia in the Kremlin. Donskoy was sure that Moscow would resist Tokhtamysh and he himself went to Pereyaslavl to collect Pereyaslavl, Suzdal and Beloozersk regiments. On August 23, the advanced Horde units approached Moscow and burned the suburbs. On August 24, the main forces besieged Moscow. For three days, the Horde unsuccessfully threw themselves on the walls, and finally resorted to the insidious reception that was usual for them. Tokhtamysh sent to the gates of the Nizhny Novgorod princes Basil and Semyon, the sons of Dmitry of Suzdal. Ostey went to the negotiations accompanied by the clergy; he was captured and killed, the spiritual ones were "stripped off," Horde forces burst into the open gates. Having seized Moscow, Tokhtamysh dispersed the detachments through the volosts. Robbed: Yuryev, Dmitrov, Mozhaisk. Under Volokolamsk detachments clashed with the army, which was collected by Vladimir Andreevich, the Horde were cut down in a short section. Learning of this, Tokhtamysh gathered scattered troops and rushed away as soon as he arrived, not wanting to meet either Vladimir Andreyevich or Dmitry Donskoy, who moved his army from Kostroma to Moscow. Thus ended Tokhtamysh's campaign against Moscow in 1382. The Horde again managed to prevent the excessive strengthening of one of the states of Eastern Europe, the Moscow, which, after the Battle of Kulikovo, entered the path of intensive integration with the Western Russian feudal lords of the Lithuanian-Russian principality. Thus, the conditions were again created for restoring the balance necessary for the Horde between Moscow and Vilna, the center of the Lithuanian principality. But what became characteristic, the Horde politicians very soon not only stopped the invasions of Moscow, but also began to support it.

Moscow and Vilna, Dmitry and Yagailo were fueled by Horde politicians - they increased the intensity of their rivalry, and at the same time fueled the sentiments of the princes in these two great principalities. As a result, in 1383, Veliky Novgorod was withdrawn from the influence of Moscow, and Yagailo, in turn, had to make territorial concessions to the Order.

The concluded Moscow-Lithuanian Treaty of 1384 was interesting because it actually recognized the leading role of Dmitry Donskoy. Under these conditions, the Horde and the Order intensified their financial and political pressure. The Horde acted through Novgorod, but the Order changed tactics and promoted the unification of Jagail and Vitovt, an ally of the Crusaders. On May 19, 1389, Dmitry Donskoy died in Moscow; on August 19, Vasily I Dmitrievich entered the throne of Moscow. In the summer of 1390, the wedding of Vasily and Sophia Vitovtovna was held in a solemn ceremony. In Eastern Europe, Vasily, Vitovt and Kiprian, who became Metropolitan on October 1, 1389, are trying to replace the Polish-Catholic colonization of the Lithuanian and Russian lands with the consolidation of Russian forces around Moscow, this was undertaken immediately after the Kulikovo victory. But in the course of the emerging historical process again closely joined the events in the Horde. A new stage in the history of the Golden Horde coincided with the death of Dmitry. Once Tokhtamysh came out of obedience to Timur and began to lay claim to the territories under his control. The confrontation began. Immediately after the death of Dmitry Donskoy, Tokhtamysh issued a label for the reign of Vladimir to his son, Basil I, and strengthened it, transferring to him the Nizhny Novgorod principality and a number of cities.

Tokhtamysh, meanwhile, tossed about in contradictions of the Horde policy in Russia, and on the Terek River in 1395 Timur's troops defeated Tokhtamysh, massacred him for his duality. After the battle on the Terek, the invincible "god of war" moved his troops through the Volga region and Dnieper to Moscow, but after standing for 15 days in Yelets, he turned away.

It should be noted that just 15 years after the Battle of Kulikovo, which demonstrated the superiority of Russian politics and Russian military art over the Horde and in many ways decisively weakened the political and economic influence of the Tatar-Mongol yoke in North-Eastern Russia, the Central Asian commander had to firmly ponder over than to engage in battle with the Moscow troops. Timur went to his limits, dividing the Volga Horde between his appointees. Meanwhile, the internal processes of consolidation of the Russian forces after the Kulikov victory had already gone out of the control of the Horde and any third force. The rapprochement between Vasily I and his father-in-law continued. Metropolitan Cyprian put a lot of energy on this. It must be assumed that he was the church leader who was needed by the emerging historical process.

A significant stage in Russian history is the reign of Basil II the Dark. From the beginning of the reign in 1425 and until 1462, he had to constantly defend his rights and fight for power, with the result that he was even blinded. The activities of this prince allowed to preserve the Russian lands for which the Lithuanian principality claimed. Repeatedly he had to enter into open confrontation with the Golden Horde. During the reign of Basil II begins the independence of the Russian Orthodox Church.

Russia suffered many devastations in the first half of the great reign of Vasily the Dark. Calling on the service of the Horde prince Kashim and applauding him Gorodets Meschersky, the Grand Duke had at his disposal an ally who was able to provide him with political and military assistance in defending Moscow Russia from the Horde raids, and at the same time to some extent participate in the centralization of Vladimir princedoms

The last decade of the reign of Vasily the Dark revealed to us a sovereign who established state power over all of North-Eastern Russia. Mozhaisk, Serpukhov, partly Novgorod, Pskov and Ryazan. He settled his business with Vasily II and the Horde. The collapse weakened the Horde, strengthening of Moscow and its troops kept the Khans from raids.

Autocracy in Northeast Russia was established in time. A new force appeared in the historical arena - the Ottoman Empire. By 1453, no European state could no longer reckon with the Turkish sultans in its policy.

Roman curia under the guise of the salvation of Christianity decided to infiltrate into Russia. The Vatican approved Isidor, the protege of Rome, as Metropolitan of All Russia, and rejected Archbishop Jonah, sent by Vasily II to Ryazan. In 1449, a peace treaty was signed between Basil the Dark and the new Polish King Casimir. Vasily completed the unification of the Russian principalities around Moscow. In 1462, Grand Duke Basil II died.

The next ruler of Russia was the eldest son of Vasily the Dark, Ivan III. From the earliest years, the father of the future prince was preparing him for governing the country, taking him on military campaigns and meetings. Being a clever but capricious politician, Ivan III led a tough domestic and foreign policy. By the end of his life, Ivan III concentrated in his hands immense power, which no European sovereign possessed.

The epoch of Ivan III is the epoch of the most complicated work of Russian diplomacy, the epoch of the strengthening of the Russian army necessary for the defense of the Russian state. The first conquest of Ivan III was the Kazan Khanate, in 1467 distemper in Kazan gave the Moscow prince a pretext for intervention. The first campaign on Kazan Tsarevich Kashima failed. In the spring of 1469 and in the summer of the same year there were 2 more campaigns. But further hostilities stopped, for the Novgorod affairs began. On December 13, 1470, the Novgorod lord Jonah died, firmly holding the side of Moscow. In the spring of 1471, Ivan III embarked on a march on Novgorod, who withdrew to Lithuania in a year. The campaign ended with the return of Moscow's former influence on Novgorod and a large buyout from the Novgorod boyars who wanted independence. The course of the whole "Novgorod affair" in 1471 showed that the idea of transferring Novgorod under the authority of King Casimir is just an adventure, which has no roots in the popular environment.

Having completed the first stage of the conquest of Novgorod and the understanding that this "Novgorod case" was not over, Ivan III took up Horde affairs. In order to neutralize Casimir, Ivan makes a witty and completely unpredictable maneuver. He marries Sophia Palaeologus - the niece of the emperor of Byzantium, who died in the walls of Constantinople.

The new pretext for pressure on Novgorod was the accession of Vasily Ananin, who was reaching out to Lithuania. October 22, 1475 Ivan went to Novgorod. On November 21, he entered Novgorod, on November 26, the Grand Prince's Court was held, after which Ananin and his assistants were immediately captured.

At that time, in 1476, the son of the Great Horde Khan Ahmat Janibek sat on the Khan's throne in Crimea. An anti-Moscow triumvirate was created: Akhmat, Janibek, Casimir. Immediately entering into negotiations with Akhmatov, in 1476, Ivan accepts from him a label for a great reign. By 1478 there was a moment to complete the affairs with Novgorod: the Sultan of the Ottoman Empire began a war with Janibek and Akhmat. November 27, Ivan III stood with his troops at the walls of the city. The formal reason for this was the complaint of Novgorod, who reached Moscow. Already on February 14, Ivan moved back, but the veche bell, the symbol of Novgorod sovereignty, also moved back with him. The problem of Novgorod was solved.

THE PERIOD OF UNIFICATION OF THE RUSSIAN LANDS

In 1492, Ivan III officially began to magnify "the sovereign of all Russia." But back in 1480, Ivan III began to prepare the political ground for the overthrow of the Horde yoke. As soon as Moscow received from Dikigo Pole the exact news that Khan Akhmat with all his might goes to the Don, the Grand Duke set up regiments on the Oka. Khan Akhmat, having learned that strong regiments were set up on the Oka, went to Kaluga to join up with Casimir. Having determined the direction of the Horde campaign, Ivan III intercepted it on the River Ugra. Moscow, meanwhile, was besieged. Akhmat threatened to launch an offensive when the ice forges the Ugra. On October 26, Ugra stood up. Stood and Akhmat. On November 11, Khan Akhmat, despite the fact that all the Ugra crossings were open, turned away. He rushed into the race through the Lithuanian parishes of his ally Casimir.

November 11, 1480, the day of the departure of Khan Akhmat from the banks of the Ugra, is considered to be the day of the complete liberation of the Russian land and the Russian people from the Horde yoke, from any dependence on the khans of the Golden Horde.

The beginning of the XVI century is associated with the rule of Vasily III - a strong and far-sighted politician. From 1502 to 1533, as a result of his reign, not only the sole power of the prince was consolidated, but the process of centralization of the Russian lands around Moscow ended. Ivan IV, who came to replace him, was not able to govern the country due to his young age, so the main power was at first in the hands of his mother Elena Glinskaya, and after her death passed to the participants of the Seven Boyars.

A difficult childhood reflected in the character of the young ruler, and at the age of 15, upon assuming the throne, he freely controlled the fate and lives of his subjects. The first half of his more than half-century rule was associated with significant successes in domestic and foreign policy. After the wedding of Ivan IV to the kingdom in 1547, the most important reforms of state bodies, the judicial system, the army, the church followed. The formation of the Russian autocracy in the sixteenth century was accompanied by its success in the field of centralization of the state and the revitalization of foreign policy. The growth of international prestige of the Moscow state was also promoted by a significant expansion of its territory due to successful conquest campaigns and the colonization of new lands in the east. The rest of the reign is characterized by total terror against the population, which towards the end of the king's life led to a significant decline, both in culture and in the economy of the country. Anyway, during the reign of Ivan the Terrible, the country's territory increased by 2 times, and the state retained its independence under the pressure of external enemies.

After the death of the king in 1584, accumulated problems led to a prolonged confusion. Despite the existence of legitimate heirs, the royal duties were performed by Boris Godunov. The energetic beginning in the management of the country, which pursued the goal of overcoming the crisis, soon changed into a policy of persecution and, in the end, only aggravated the difficult situation. The story of the deceased prince Dmitriy and the deceased legitimate heir Fedor finally undermined the authority of Godunov and did not allow him to permanently establish himself as a king. (Pushkarev, 2002).

For a long time, the country could not get out of distemper. The main reasons for the problems were the absence of a legal heir, candidates for the throne appearing against this background, referred to as prince Dmitriy and the Swedish - Polish intervention. The short-sighted policy of the then ruling Vasily Shuisky led to the fact that as a result of the invasion of the Polish troops in 1610, the boyars recognized the victory of Poland and agreed with the rule of the Polish king Vladislav. The patience of the people ended in 1612. As a result of the militia assembled by the Nizhny Novgorod Minin and Pozharsky Polish invaders were driven out of the country. Less than a year later, Mikhail Romanov was elected the Tsar at the Zemsky Sobor. His rule was connected with the stabilization of the situation in the country.

From 1645, Alexey Mikhailovich Romanov received the blessing on reign. During his reign, many controversial events occurred, among which

- Split the church in 1651;
- War of 1654-1667 with the Commonwealth for the Ukrainian territory;
- Peasant Uprisings: The salt revolt of 1648, the Novgorod-Pskov uprising of 1650, the copper revolt of 1662 and the war of 1667-1671.

The next king was Fedor Alekseevich, who for the 6-year term of government managed to cancel the practice of parochialism and win the war with the Turks in 1676-1681.

After the death of Fyodor in 1682, the struggle for power began between princess Sophia Alekseevna and supporters of Tsarevich Ivan and Peter, which ended in 1689 with a joint reign of the latter up to 1696.

Up to 1725, Russia was headed by Peter the Great, named Great for his reformist views. A number of changes were made domestically. From January 1, 1700, a new chronology was adopted in Russia. In 1703, St. Petersburg was founded, which 10 years later became the new capital of the country. And in the course of an active foreign policy and the Northern War of 1700-1721. newly obtained access to the Baltic Sea.

The reforms of Peter I encompassed all spheres of state and public life, determining the development of our country for a long historical perspective. They were aimed at maximizing centralization in the management of the state with its decisive influence on the life of all sectors of society and tight regulation of all its parties. After the death of Peter I, the Russian Empire entered the era of palace coups.

Empress was proclaimed the widow of Peter I Catherine. In this case, the actual administration of affairs was entrusted to the Secret Council. According to her testament, the throne was handed over to Peter II, but his rule lasted only 3 years and in 1730 the country again faced the question of the heir.

The next ruler of Russia proclaimed Princess Anne of Courland, and the period of its ten-year reign, due to the strong influence of the favorite Biron, began to be called "Bironovshchina". After the death of Anna Ioannovna, the throne was to be ceded to her nephew, Ivan Antonovich, but after another palace coup, the younger daughter of Peter the Great, Elizabeth, withdrew.

Despite a good education and a lively mind, Elizaveta Petrovna did not pay enough attention to public affairs, shifting this responsibility to the Senate. However, in 20 years of government, the situation in Russia has stabilized, the central power has become stronger, and various forms of art, science and education have received special development. Due to the absence of children, in 1762 the reins of government were transferred to Peter III (Sakharov, 1997).

The pro-Western policy and open love of Peter III to Prussia, as a result of which all the achievements of the Seven Years War were returned to the losing side, caused a negative reaction among the people and closest subjects. In 1762, at the next coup, Peter was overthrown and killed, and his place was taken by his wife, nee Princess Sophia Frederik Augusta of Anhalt-Tserpt, who took the name Ekaterina Alekseevna after baptism (Semenikova, 2004).

The 34-year rule of Catherine II was one of the most prosperous in the history of Russia. At that time, science, art, power strengthened, the borders of the empire expanded, and competent international politics was conducted. Much attention was paid to the development of education in the country. Although the empress led a rather progressive policy, discontent among the peasants, which resulted in the Pugachev rebellion of 1771-1774, was brewing in the country.

During the reign of Catherine II, Russia led an active foreign policy. The country sought to solve the problem of relations with the Ottoman Empire.

At the same time, the difficult situation in Poland gave Russia quite good chances to return the territories lost as far back as the 13th - 15th centuries.

The peace treaty with Turkey was signed in 1774 after many brilliant victories won by Russian commanders. The most famous of these was the Battle of Chesme. Russia moved the territory between the Dnieper and the Southern Bug, the fortress of Kerch and Azov. Crimea became independent of Turkey and soon became part of Russia. This happened in 1783. The Russian-Turkish war of 1787–1791 became victorious for Russia. Borders were transferred to the Dniester (from the Southern Bug).

At the end of the XVIII century, Russia was able to finally establish itself in the status of a world power. The country joined the anti-French coalition in 1782. The reason for this was the revolutionary events in France. Planned campaign in Europe under the command of Suvorov. The death of Empress Catherine II did not allow to realize these plans. But, the Italian campaign of Suvorov nevertheless took place in 1799. However, Paul I, who ascended the throne, considered allied relations with France more advantageous for the country (Troitsk, 2003).

The reign of the son of Catherine Paul I, was short and ended in 1801. From 1801 to 1825, the country was ruled by his son Alexander I, during the years of whose rule the most important victory was won against the Napoleonic troops in the Patriotic War of 1812. The main contribution to the defeat of the French army was made by the pupil of the famous commander A.V. Suvorov, Commander-in-Chief of the Russian Army M.I. Kutuzov.

CONCLUSION

Thus, the era of the baptism of Russia coincided with the period of the formation of statehood, when the establishment of a firm autocracy of the Grand Duke became a vital necessity. A further period of state development in the history of our country was not an easy one. The rulers come by fire and sword to prove the state consistency and this they always managed.

REFERENCES

Ershov, B. A. (2012). Historiographical aspects of the relationship between the Russian Orthodox Church and state structures in the provinces of the Central Chernozem region in the XIX -early XX centuries. *Bulletin of the Voronezh State Technical University. Series Humanities, 8*(11), 188–192.

Ershov, B. A. (2013). Russian Orthodox Church in the structure of public administration in the XIX - early XX centuries: Monograph. Voronezh State Technical University, Russia.

Ershov, B. A., Ashmarov, I. A., Drobyshev, A. V., Zhdanova, T. A., & Buravlev, I. A. (2017). Property and Land Relations of Russian Orthodox Church and State in Russia. *The European Proceedings of Social and Behavioural Sciences,* 324-331.

Gorinov, M. M. (1995). History of Russia: from antiquity up to now. The Highest School. (in Russian)

Gorinov, M. M. (1997). History of Russia: The manual. *Under the Editorship.* (in Russian)

Klyuchevsky, V. O. (1995). *Russian history: full course of lectures: in 3 princes – Prince 3.* Academic Press. (in Russian)

Kornilov, A. A. (2004). *Course of the Russian history of the 19th century.* Academic Press. (in Russian)

Pavlenko, N. I. (2000). The history of Russia from the most ancient times to 1861: studies for higher education institutions. *Under the Editorship,* 473-519. (in Russian)

Platonov, S. F. (2005). *A course of lectures on the Russian history.* Academic Press. (in Russian)

Pushkarev, S. G. (2002). Review of the Russian history, 343-354. (in Russian)

Sakharov, A. N. (1997). The history of Russia since the beginning of XVIII until the end of the 19th century. Institute of the Russian history of RASP. (in Russian)

Semenikova, L. I., Golovkina, N. L., Sdobnina, T. V., Cherkesova, N. N. (2004). National history: abstract of lectures: studies. *The Settlement for Higher Education Institutions,* 134-144. (in Russian)

Semennikova, L. I. (2000). Russia in the international community of civilizations. Bryansk, "Italics." (in Russian)

Troitsk, N. A. (2003). *Russia in the 19th century: course of lectures: studies.* Academic Press. (in Russian)

Chapter 2
Social and Economic Factors of Development

Bogdan Ershov
Voronezh State Technical University, Russia

Natalia Muhina
Voronezh State Technical University, Russia

Igor Asmarov
Voronezh State Institute of Arts, Russia

ABSTRACT

Russian statehood has more than a thousand-year history and traditions. It is obvious that the social, economic, and political development of the country had its direct or indirect influence on the Russian state and statehood itself. Therefore, in this chapter we separately single out the social factors of the development of Russian statehood and the economic factors of the development of Russian statehood, which stand apart from each other. Social factors in the development of Russian statehood are factors in the development of society as a single and complex organism and its social institutions. Social factors are, in essence, domestic political, because they represent the political and spiritual state of the elite and the people, the established system of social relations, internal social contradictions, and social conflicts. The economic factors of the development of Russian statehood are divided into external and internal ones. External economic factors are the proximity or remoteness from the trade routes, and the qualitative and quantitative composition of the country's exports and imports. Internal economic factors are the achieved material state of society, the availability of natural resources and their involvement in the economy, the availability of transport and production infrastructure and its development, and economic crises.

DOI: 10.4018/978-1-5225-9985-2.ch002

INTRODUCTION

Since the beginning of the X century, there were significant changes not only in the political, but also in the social system and in the economic life of Russia.

In 882, Novgorod Prince Oleg united all the Eastern Slavic lands into a single state, Russia. Kievan Rus was the largest and most powerful state of medieval Europe. Its territory stretched from the Baltic to the Black Sea, from the Carpathians to the Volga, and covered approximately 800 thousand square kilometers. In fact, it was the empire in which they lived, for various calculations, from 3 to 12 million people. It existed from the 9th to the middle of the 12th century and broke up into 15 separate lands that existed as sovereign states or independent principalities.

The formation of the Kiev state was a factor that accelerated the formation of private land ownership. X-XI centuries. - a period of intensive development, which took place in two directions. First, with the formation of the state, there was a process of conquering the territories of neighboring communities, the formation of the state, represented by the prince, of land ownership. Secondly, the economic differentiation in the society increased.

A number of researchers claim that in the princely period (9th – first half of the 12th centuries) feudalism existed in the guise of the state system. It was characterized by the increased role of princely power, which developed economic relations.

In the first stages of the formation of feudalism, the feudal class as a whole became the supreme owner of the land. At the head of the corporation of feudal lords became the prince, who was, in such images, the supreme feudal owner of the state territory.

The right of land ownership belonged exclusively to the feudal class. The princely, boyar and church land tenure was the estate property, which had a hierarchical and at the same time conditional character. The landowners of the feudal principalities were vassals of the Grand Duke. Large landowners, in turn, had smaller vassals. With the growth of feudal relations, by seizing peasant communal lands, princely, boyar and monastic feudal land tenure was formed. Kievan Rus had property in the form of patrimonial land tenure, where the labor of peasants — serfs and serfs was exploited. Along with the different categories of feudal-dependent peasants in slaves, slave labor was used on a small scale. In the era of early feudalism, there were still many free peasant serfs living on communal land. However, a large patrimony, princely, boyar and monastic, threatened communal land tenure more and more.

At the end of the X-beginning of the XI century, Russia enters into the swath of completion of the disintegration of the tribal system. A new organization based on territorial links is being born. Already in the 9th century, the features of pre-feudal social relations were quite clearly defined. Further relations during the X-XI centuries demanded restructuring and the form of the state. With the active assistance of the superstructure, large land tenure has grown and strengthened on the ground. The political role of landowning nobility has risen greatly. The form of exploitation of the dependent peasantry has changed. New urban centers were clearly indicated. Various political organizations contributed to the strengthening of the economic and political position of the landowning nobility. By the end of the 9th century, one can speak of the existence of the early feudal Old Russian state, which is continuously growing during the 10th and the first half of the 11th centuries.

Simultaneously with the development of social relations, which gave rise to the exploitation of the personally free direct producers in the state by the ruling class, the social and economic system based on the exploitation of the dependent population — the master economy — took shape in the 9th and 11th centuries. In the 9th-11th centuries, the process of the formation of the master's landed property took place, which was the economic basis for the exploitation of the dependent population in the patrimony. In ancient Russia, domination began with small land areas. At this time, the courtyard arises as a complex housing complex, which was one of the factors of the economic stability of the princely and non-princely economy. The operation of the princely and boyar households required additional sources of labor, which turned the master's court into a center not only for economic but also for social and economic activity. The materials relating to the X century, contains data on the complex composition of the princely domain. It consisted of courtyards, villages, cities, unfortified settlements of urban-type "places". The courtyards were the center of the economy serving and local nobility.

In the 9th-10th centuries, the establishment of the state's supreme ownership of the land took place, which expressed the system of land and socio-economic relations between the state and subordination within Ancient Russia, which ensured the enrichment and reproduction of the ruling class. The process of external and internal East Slavic colonization in the X-XI centuries is explained by the growing feudal oppression.

The establishment of state supreme ownership of land is the main means of production and the "universal subject of human labor." It was crucial in the process of class formation of Ancient Russia, determining the socio-economic situation of the peasantry, as an aggregate of small producers in agriculture, as a single class of society, regardless of differences in economic systems: landowning, hunting and farming, cattle breeding, established in accordance with natural conditions.

Given the high degree of development of crafts in Russia, some historians emphasize the commercial orientation of its economy. Others, in contrast to them, argue that agriculture is the basis of the economy in Russia. Agriculture has become the main occupation of the population of the Eastern Slavs. In Kievan Rus, it continued to develop, acquiring new organizational forms. In the area of Kiev and Novgorod, already in the X-XI centuries, the plowed system became the leading system of agriculture. The profound changes in the main branch of the economy, agriculture, led to no less profound changes in the relations of production of our ancestors, the gradual emergence of feudal relations of production. From about the 9th century, the Eastern Slavs established a feudal mode of production (in the presence of a multi-pattern economy), which opened up much room for the development of production forces.

Ancient Russia knew many grain crops: millet, wheat, rye, barley, oats, peas, as well as flax, etc. Numerous vegetable, bean and industrial crops were cultivated as well. The agricultural economy of the forest-steppe zone in the IX-XI centuries reached a significant degree of development. As a result, it was possible to alienate the surplus product and conduct expanded reproduction, which created prerequisites for the growth of property and social stratification of the rural population, for an increase in the rate of exploitation by landowners within the state and stately farms. Along with land ownership, other types of economic activity were also common, in particular cattle breeding. The Eastern Slavs in the IX-X centuries had all kinds of domestic animals: large and small cattle (fattening cattle the peasant provided himself not only with meat and milk, but also with skin for making clothes and shoes), pigs, horses and poultry. The accumulation of livestock could also contribute to increasing income inequality. Hunting and fishing also played a role in the farm. In the forests there were many different animals and wild birds - squirrels, beavers, martens, foxes, sables, bison, elks, deer, goats, wild boars, hares, swans, cranes, ducks, geese, quails. Furs, honey and wax were exported in large quantities to the foreign market. They peasants paid their taxes.

Most recent excavations have confirmed that in the 9th-10th centuries in Ukraine, the plow, plow, plow, harrow, shovel, sickle and scythe were used for tillage and crop production. Arable implements developed more slowly in the forest zone. Changes in the types of arable tools were determined by latitudinal natural conditions. Therefore, the level of their development limited the norms of exploitation. The economic changes that took place in the 9th and 11th centuries indicate a significant progress of the productive forces of the Eastern Slavs. During this period, iron was widely used in the manufacture of agricultural implements (ticks, crescents, sickles), plows appeared. Farmers used a variety of tools for secondary tillage, rakes and forks were used. These tools expanded the possibilities of agricultural production, the basis of the economy of the Eastern Slavs.

The emergence of the Slavs of Kiev, Novgorod and Smolensk indicates the growth of the craft. The population of these cities mainly consisted of small traders and artisans. So, from 40 to 60 different crafts were presented in Kiev. The most important among them were carpentry, blacksmithing, humbling, pottery. Iron, metallurgical, jewelry and ceramic production was developed. Already in those days, the blacksmiths owned "forging gold and silver", welding iron and steel, splitting metal, inlaying non-ferrous metals. Craftsmen made: rala, plows, sickles, axes, swords, arrows, shields, chain mail, locks, key, bracelets and rings of gold and silver. The craft was developed, both in the structure of the prince and the feudal lord's economy, and on a free landing basis. With the emergence of cities, two forms of crafts develop - urban and rural. The main part of the artisans are concentrated in the cities, where most of the trade was concentrated. Cities had a great influence on the development of the craft; in turn, the allocation of craft in no small measure contributed to the transformation of some settlements in the city. The development of cities as a handicraft and shopping center is, above all, an indicator of growth in the domestic market. The period of Kievan Rus is a time of relatively intensive development of the craft. The artisans were already a special group of the population. The urban craft during the 9th-11th centuries was highly developed. The following professions of artisans of this period can be noted: blacksmiths and gunsmiths, jewelers, foundry workers, forged, spearmen, carpenters, carpenters, bone carvers, chasers, weavers, potters, etc. If in the 9th-10th centuries only 26 cities were known, in the 11th century- 62 cities. Products of artisans found sales not only within the country, but also abroad: in Poland, the Czech Republic, Sweden and other countries.

As a result, commodity production arose. It existed in Russia at the early stage of feudalism. To a greater extent, its appearance is associated with the growth of crafts and cities. Feudal lords sold on the market products of unpaid labor. Commodity production reaches a new level in the era of Kievan Rus, when the minting of its own Russian coin began. Commercial capital acts as an intermediary in the exchange of the surplus product assigned by the feudal lords in the exchange of the products of the peasants and the handicraft population. Feudal Russia is characterized not only by the existence of the domestic market, but also by developed foreign trade. The size of the market depended on the degree of specialization of social labor. The selection of crafts, the emergence and growth of cities contributed to the expansion of the domestic market. The economic importance of cities grew due to the growth of productive forces. At the first stages of feudalism, the producers themselves were directly involved in trade; artisans, peasants; feudal lords sold products obtained in the form of pre-capitalist rent. In addition to handicrafts, agricultural products (rye, oats) were supplied to the market, and salt, fish, honey, etc. were also sold. Thus, peasant and patrimonial farms were involved in commodity relations. Foreign merchants also performed in the inner city markets. During this period, there was monetary (mainly in the cities) barter. For Ancient Russia, the connection of trading with churches was typical: the clergy, along with the princes, were engaged in trade. The emergence of foreign trade relations of the Eastern Slavs with other nations go back centuries. The Volga and its tributaries were the main artery along which trade with the Arabs took place. Trade of the Slavs with the Arabs lasted until about the X century. In the 9th century, trade in Ancient Russia with Byzantium, Kherson and Constantinople intensified. Of great importance for foreign trade, for the growth of cities such as Kiev and Novgorod, had the famous path "from the Varangians to the Greeks." Ancient Russia imported silk and gold fabrics, cloth, velvet, weapons, art craft items, church utensils, spices, fruit and wine, paint, horses, salt, precious and non-ferrous metals. Kievan Rus led a relatively broad foreign trade. The appearance of merchants, which marks the emergence of the third social division of labor, the introduction of metallic money, the formation of private ownership of land are important steps in the development of commodity production. In the economy of Kievan Rus trade, in particular foreign trade with Arabs, Greeks, Transcaucasia, the peoples of Central Asia and Western Europe (the Czech Republic, Poland, Scandinavia, etc.), played a significant role.

Feudal rent included, as a rule, the entire surplus product of the dependent peasantry, and sometimes part of the necessary. Feudal rent was appropriated by the landowner, but part of it was received by the state in the form of taxes. Rent in terms of feudalism is closely connected with government taxes, finances, etc. The size of rent and taxes often coincided, and it is impossible to separate them, especially at the early stage of development of feudalism, because at that time there was no sharp line between state ownership of land and the personal property of princes. Forms of rent (developmental, natural, monetary) correspond to the various stages of development of the feudal-serf mode of production. Historical documents (although not numerous) indicate that in Kievan Rus the primitive form of labor rent prevailed.

The economic universality of the feudal fiefdom, its complex composition (courtyards, villages, townships, cities in the domain), a significant differentiation of the dependent population in the master's economy caused various forms of exploitation in German labor rent, natural and monetary rent. As a result, the needs of the owners of domains and estates were satisfied, which was the main economic stimulus in the organization by the dominant class of their own farms.

Kiev state had a relatively developed monetary system. As the social division of labor grows, the role of money is increasingly shifting to noble metals. Coinage began in Kievan Rus earlier than in some large European states in the X-XI centuries. The presence of own coins in Kievan Rus is one of the evidence of its large role in political and economic life at that time. Money circulation existed primarily in ancient Russian cities with more developed trade, handicrafts, usurious credit, etc. The presence of money circulation can be judged by levying tribute, taxes, the accumulation of precious metals from feudal lords, etc. As commodity production grew, functions of money developed, such as measures of value, means of circulation, means of accumulation, means of payment, and world money. Money as a medium of circulation and world money were widely used in Kievan Rus; they turned into profitable capital.

First of all, it is not only the high level of Russian culture of the IX-XI centuries that catches the eye, but also its wide distribution. In Russia at this time there were a lot of artists. In the Russian cities in the X-XI centuries, there were magnificent buildings. The brilliant and deep culture of Kievan Rus is the result of the centuries-old life of a great and creative people. Thus, the economy of Kievan Rus reaches a relatively high level. The population of the state was about 4-5 million people. Kievan Rus knew already developed craft. Trade played a large part in the economy, in particular foreign trade with Arabs, Greeks, and peoples of Western Europe. In addition to Kiev, trade relations were established by other cities of Ancient Rus. The economic relations of Kievan Rus were very complex: it combined feudal relations, and the degree of feudalization in certain parts of the country was uneven. The era of early feudalism is characterized by the expansion of feudal relations and, as a result, the reduction of the number of peasant communes, the conversion of tribute into a primitive form of labor rent. At the same time, this is the era of relatively rapid growth of crafts and trade.

From the end of the 12th to the first half of the 16th century, a period of feudal fragmentation took place in Russia, the causes of which were:

1. The division of ancient Russian lands between the heirs of the Grand Duke Yaroslav the Wise;
2. The natural character of the old Russian economy;
3. The growth of boyar estates;
4. The growth and strengthening of cities that demanded political and economic independence;
5. The loss of its great significance of the route from the "Varangians to the Greeks" as a result of the movement of the main transport and trade routes to the Mediterranean;
6. More frequent nomad raids from the south.

In the second half of the 12th century, the population of the southwestern Kyivan lands began to abandon the developed areas and move to the northeast, between the Oka and Volga rivers. This was due primarily to security, because in such remote places it was possible to hide from external enemies, as well as the opportunity to acquire free, fairly fertile land. There was a gradual assimilation of the Slavic tribes with the local Finno-Ugric tribes, resulting in the formation of the Russian nation.

In the middle of the 12th century, the Vladimir-Suzdal principality, headed by Yury Dolgoruky, the son of Vladimir Monomakh, was formed here. In the new region formed an active rural population with a very small proportion of the urban population. People engaged in craft, fishing, hunting. Trade, in contrast to Kievan Rus, did not have the same influence; therefore, the economy remained natural for a long time.

As a result of the Russian colonization of the Volga-Oka lands, other forms of relations between the prince and the population began to be created here. The prince acted as the owner - the owner of land, disposed of them, bequeathed to his heirs.

From the 12th-13th centuries, the hierarchical structure of land tenure was established in the feudal land ownership of the Vladimir-Suzdal principality. At the head of the hierarchical ladder was the eldest prince, who could transfer part of his land to conditional possession of vassals in exchange for providing them with certain assistance, for example, participating in military campaigns.

The heirs of the eldest prince, who received the full ownership of the land, became "appanage princes", and their possessions were called "inheritances". Such hereditary landowners became the sovereign masters in their inheritance in relation to the farmers living in their territory, they had the legal authority to collect taxes, settle disputes, etc. Such a vassal system firmly held power over the peasants.

In these conditions, the main privileged form of land ownership was still the boyar patrimony, which remained a large, independent economic unit. As a rule, farms of vassals dependent on the patrimonial estates were concentrated around it. Boyar virtually dominated over large territories and farmers who lived there. The farms remained almost completely natural, all basic needs were met by the products that were produced inside the fiefdoms.

The clergy began to play a large role not only in the ideological, but also in the economic life of the country. Church landownership in their size did not yield to the boyars' patrimonies. Churches and monasteries, as well as the feudal lords, seized communal lands, attacking the rights of peasants. Moreover, their possessions were not broken up and assigned to the church forever.

During the period of domination of the patrimonial estate, local or conditional land tenure became more and more prominent. Princes, boyars, monasteries are increasingly invited to his military service of various people: the younger prince and boyar children, ruined feudal lords. For the performance of the service, landowners gave them plots of land - "estates" - for conditional use for the period of service to the owner of the land. After the end of the life of the estate could be selected. From such invited, a new class of "service people" was formed, which in relation to the peasantry acquired the same rights as the feudal lords. Frequently, the feudal lords sent service people to their remote villages and villages as managers, organizers of production, and for this they were forced to give them part of their property in the form of an estate under certain conditions. Later, the feudal lords began to give servicemen as a reward the right of them to collect taxes ("stern") from the peasants, that is, to engage in "feeding", which meant an increase in the economic dependence of the population. Servants made up the so-called "courtyard" of princes and boyars, so later they were called "nobles".

The main sector of the economy remained agriculture. The development of new territories gradually expanded to the north to the White Sea and to the northeast to the Urals. The main labor force of both fiefdoms and estates were dependent peasants, which can be divided into several large groups (categories). One of them was the "old residents", who for several generations had lived on the lands of this feudal lord and were closely associated with it. Legally they were free, economically more and more dependent on the feudal lord, turning into serfs.

The next group consisted of the so-called "newcomers," or "new soldiers," who had recently moved from other estates or estates. After some time, they, as a rule, fell into the category of debtors, since they could not pay the feudal lord fully and on time, which, in turn, led them to enslavement.

Monastic peasants were divided into two main groups: "big" and "pedestrians". Larger ones are stronger owners, pedestrians are poor peasants who had neither horses nor tools, and performed various household chores: they threshed grain, prepared malt, baked bread, looked after cattle, etc.

Nevertheless, the complete legal and economic enslavement of the peasants has not yet taken shape, since this process was opposed by a fairly strong community. In addition, the peasants had the right to move to new lands, to other feudal lords. And since there was still no strong centralized power, there were no uniform legal norms in the country for enslaving the peasants.

The main form of economic dependence of the peasants on landowners was a natural rent (rent products). This included agricultural products and household products. The amount of the rent was determined by the customs ("antiquity") and was stipulated in advance by the parties, so the peasants could increase the area of crops in order to achieve better results and after calculating more products left for their needs and for exchange. In addition, the peasants carried out a number of duties, that is, there was a corvée, or an idle (labor rent), but it had not played a noticeable role anywhere except in the monastic farms. Money rent occupied a very small place, since market relations and money circulation were still very poorly developed.

Along with agriculture, some progress was also observed in urban handicraft production. The development of the iron industry, in particular, in Novgorod, in the Moscow region (Serpukhov, Kashira). Blacksmithing continued to play a prominent role, especially in the production of cold arms (swords, sabers) and protective military armor (shields, mail, armor). There were workshops for casting church bells and artillery cannons.

Since the 14th century, the mass construction of stone and brick buildings, mainly church and monastic, began, so the profession of a bricklayer and a builder became common. A prominent place was occupied by salt.

Particularly noticeable was the development of exchange for fairly primitive trades (Torzhok), where, along with food and agricultural goods, it was possible to buy for money or in exchange clay and wooden dishes, barrels, sledges, leather and felted shoes and other handicraft products.

But feudal fragmentation prevented the creation of an all-Russian domestic market, since in each principality, in all major cities, a large number of travel and trade duties and fees were imposed. For transportation of goods across princely borders and city gates there was a tamga or myt (myto). They took a "turnout" from those who came to the bargaining, when crossing the rivers, they took the tax "bridge" or "transportation", depending on the weight of the goods, it was necessary to pay "weight", "pood", "lift", for marking the cattle they paid "spot", for each head of livestock in the market one had to pay "horny" or "tethered", with each person accompanying the goods, it was necessary to pay "bones", for "storing goods" in commercial premises they paid "living room", etc. This practice was exacerbated by constant internecine clashes and feudal wars.

The development of domestic trade inevitably led to more active monetary circulation. But due to the lack of precious metal mining in Russia for a long time, they used imported silver and copper bullion in their domestic circulation, as well as foreign coins, in particular German, Riga, Lubeck brands, shilingami, pfenigami, etc. The Mongolian Gold Horde coins were also used. Dirgema "or" Denga "(" ringing "). Hence the term "money" in Russian. These were small silver coins with Arabic inscriptions. After the Battle of Kulikovo in 1380, Moscow's Prince Dmitry Donskoy began peresekanivat Mongolian coins. Gradually, the dengue became a small bargaining chip, common in many princedoms of Russia. It was made from the ruble hryvnia. Silver ingot weighing 200 g was pulled into a wire, cut into small pieces, each of them was flattened and minted coins of irregular shape. From the ruble it turned out in Moscow 200 denezhek-tits, in Novgorod —216 Novgorod, and so they did in virtually every principality, which, of course, did not contribute to the unification of the Russian lands.

As in the Old Russian state, in the period of feudal fragmentation in Russia, internal trade played a less prominent role than external. Already at the end of the 13th and the beginning of the 14th centuries, foreign economic relations revived again. A special place among the Russian cities was occupied by Novgorod the Great, in which numerous trade relations with various countries of Western Europe were concentrated. Novgorod carried out these connections through the Baltic lands. Especially actively traded Novgorod merchants with the North German trade union - Hansa, whose trading posts were located in many north-western cities. Fur, flax, leather, wood, tar, honey, wax, whale and walrus tallow and other goods were still exported to Novgorod through Western Europe. Imported goods consisted mainly of non-ferrous metals, fine cloth, luxury goods, salt, wine.

Already in the XII century in Novgorod there was a foreign trading post - the so-called Gothic court, which was founded by merchants from the island of Gotland. Later, the German court appeared from the Hanseatic League. In addition to foreigners, Russian merchants from many cities and principalities traded in Novgorod: Pskov, Tver, Polotsk, Smolensk, etc. At the same time, other shopping centers such as Tver and Nizhny Novgorod were developing. Through them along the Volga and the Caspian Sea, trade ties were established with the eastern and southern countries of Central Asia, Persia, and India. At the turn of the XIII-XIV centuries, the rise of Moscow began.

The unification of Russia under its authority is divided into three stages:

1. The end of the XIII century. - 1380s;
2. 1380s - 1462 g;
3. 1462 - the middle of the XVI century.

The development of the Russian economy in the XV-XVI centuries is primarily associated with the gradual enslavement of the peasants who lived in princely, boyar and church lands. Its mechanism was as follows. From year to year it became increasingly difficult for them to move to new places, because their debt to landowners grew steadily, because of crop failures and other natural disasters. Permanent loans tied their land, because not allowed to leave her. Under Ivan III in 1497, the Code of Law was published, in which periods were recorded in which the peasants could leave their masters (the week before and after St. George's day), paying them elderly. The sum of the latter at the end of the XV-beginning of the XVI century. was equal to 1 rub. (this is 1 horse, 100 poods of rye, 7 pounds of honey). Those peasants who left without paying the elderly were considered fluent and were subject to return.

The legal formalization of the dependence of the peasants on landowners took shape at the end of the 16th and 17th centuries. For this in 1582-86. "reserved summers" were established during which, it was forbidden for peasants to move to Yuryev Day. In addition, "scribal books" (based on a census of population and land) were created, in which the peasants belonged to a particular owner. Finally, "summer summaries" were established, during which the search for fugitive peasants was announced (from the beginning for five years, and then indefinite). The final legislative registration of serfdom occurred in January 1649 at the Zemsky Sobor, when the Council Code was adopted. According to him, the peasants with their family, property, etc., were declared the property of the feudal lord. The latter were given virtually unlimited judicial and administrative authority over the peasants.

By the end of the XVI century. the territory of Russia has almost doubled compared with the middle of the century, and the population was up to 7 million people.

The main branch of the Russian economy in the XVI century. there was agriculture. Hunting and fur trades are pushed to the outskirts and retain their value only in Siberia and in the North. Fisheries and beekeeping continued to develop, and during this period, they moved from primitive farming to beekeeping (organized) beekeeping.

Agriculture developed extensively - by developing new areas and increased deforestation and clearing land for arable land in the central regions of the country.

The main agricultural tool remained wooden plow; in the forest areas, a two-toothed and three-toothed plow was used. In the central regions, they began to cultivate the land with plow deer, which is a plow-type tool. The progress of the productive forces of agriculture in the conditions of invariability of labor tools was manifested mainly in the promotion of agriculture in new areas and in the spread of the three-field system. In the central regions of the country in the XVI century. the three-field with the correct alternation of winter, spring and steam fields became dominant.

For working the land with primitive tools, working animals were required. Three-plow plow and plow-roe pulled two or three horses. Therefore, the development of arable farming was accompanied by the growth of cattle breeding.

In the second half of the XVI century. began the process of colonization of the suburbs. Its two main directions stood out: to the south and southeast of Moscow and to the east - the Urals and Siberia. The empty lands of the east were called the wild field; since these outskirts of the Muscovite state were constantly subjected to raids by the Nogai and Crimean Tatars, measures were taken to reinforce and master them to strengthen the defense. Fortified points and fortresses were built along the southern border - a zasechnaya line, where people carrying border services were settled, for which they were given small plots of land. In the 60-70s of the XVI century. peasant colonization of the southern lands intensified. Landowners also rushed to the rich black earths. The government complained to them in these areas huge estates. The eastern lands of Western and Central Siberia were inhabited mainly by peasants.

The process of uniting disparate territories into a single state was accompanied by the development of cities where handicrafts and trade were concentrated. Cities overgrown with tenements in which free artisans settled. In favor of the prince, the population of the townships was borne by duty

— posadskoe ploy. By the end of the XVI century. Russia, there were about 220 cities. The largest city was Moscow with a population of 100 thousand people. In the remaining cities of Russia, there were 3-8 thousand people each. The largest Russian cities were Novgorod, Pskov, Vologda, Veliky Ustyug, Kazan, Yaroslavl, Sol Kama, Kaluga, Nizhny Novgorod, Tula, Astrakhan.

The beginning of the XVII century in the history of Russia was marked by major political and socio-economic upheavals. This time was called by historians the Troubles. The consequence of the time of troubles was a powerful regress of the economic and socio-political situation compared to that achieved by the end of the XVI century.

Ways of development of the state after the Troubles were determined by the tasks of restoring the country. The recovery process after the unrest took about three decades and was completed by mid-century.

The territory of Russia in the XVII century. compared with the 16th century, it expanded due to the inclusion of new lands of Siberia, the Southern Urals and Left-Bank Ukraine, and the further development of the Wild Field. The territory of the country was divided into counties, the number of which reached 250. The counties, in turn, were divided into townships and camps, the center of which was the village. In a number of lands, especially from among those that were recently incorporated into Russia, the former system of administrative structure remained. According to the number of inhabitants of Russia in the borders of the XVII century. ranked fourth among European states. In the 17th century, the position of Moscow Rus was in many respects better than European states. The 17th century for Europe is the time of the bloody Thirty Years War, which brought ruin, famine and extinction to people (for example, the war in Germany reduced the population from 18 million to 4 million).

In the XVII century. the foundation of the country's economy, as before, was agriculture, which was of a natural nature. The growth of agricultural production was achieved through the development of new lands, that is, through extensive research. By the middle of the XVII century. the devastation and ruin of times of unrest were overcome. And there was something to restore. In 14 counties of the center of the country in the 40s plowed land was only 42% of the previously cultivated, and the number of peasant population who fled from the horrors of timelessness decreased. The economy was recovering slowly in the conditions of preservation of traditional forms of farming, a sharply continental climate and low soil fertility in the Non-Black Earth region of the most developed part of the country. Agriculture remained the leading sector of the economy. The main tools were plow, plow, harrow, sickle. The three-field course prevailed, but the sub-section remained, especially in the north of the country. Sowed rye, oats, wheat, barley, buckwheat, peas, industrial crops, flax and hemp. The yield was self-3, in the south - self-4. The farm still had a natural character. In these conditions, the growth of production volumes was achieved due to the involvement of new lands in the economic turnover. Chernozem Region, Middle Volga Region, Siberia.

At the same time, the growth of the territory, the differences in the natural conditions caused the economic specialization of the regions of the country.

The specialization was associated with such an important process in the economy of the period under review, as the development of ¬ monetary and monetary relations. Specialization was observed not only in agriculture, but also in the craft. In the XVII century. small-scale production is distributed, i.e. the manufacture of products not on order, but on the market. Pomorie specialized in the creation of wooden products, Pskov, Novgorod, Smolensk produced linen fabrics, salt-making developed in the North, etc.

Thus, the role of merchants in the life of the country has increased. Constantly gathering fairs acquired great importance: Makaryevskaya near Nizhny Novgorod, Svenskaya Fair near Bryansk, Irbitskaya Fair in Siberia, Fair in Arkhangelsk, etc., where merchants conducted large-scale wholesale and retail trade.

Along with the development of domestic trade grew and foreign. Until the middle of the century, foreign merchants, who had exported wood, fur, hemp, potash, etc., gained enormous benefits from foreign trade. Suffice it to say that the English fleet was built from the Russian forest, and the ropes for its ships were made from Russian hemp. The center of Russian trade with Western Europe was Arkhangelsk. There were English and Dutch trade yards. Close ties were established with the countries of the East through Astrakhan, where the Indian and Persian trade yards were located.

The Russian government supported the growing merchants. In 1667, a New Trade Charter was issued, developing the provisions of the Trade Charter in 1653. A new Trade Charter increased duties on foreign goods. Foreign merchants had the right to conduct wholesale trade only in border shopping centers.

In the XVII century. the exchange of goods between individual regions of the country significantly expanded, which indicated the beginning of the formation of the all-Russian market. The merging of separate lands into a single economic system began. Growing economic ties strengthened the country's political unity.

On the basis of small-scale production, large-scale enterprises are formed, based on the division of labor and hand-made craft equipment — manufactory. In contrast to Western Europe, where the manufacture of manufactory production took place in the private sector, as capital accumulated with the owners, in Russia the state initiated the creation of manufactories. In the XVII century. In Russia, there were approximately 30 manufactories. The first state-owned manufactories appeared in the XVI century. (Pushkarsky yard, Mint). In the XVII century. metallurgical plants were built in the Urals and in the Tula region, leather factories in Yaroslavl and Kazan, Khamovny (textile) yard in Moscow.

Usually, the Nikitsa copper smelter in the Urals, built in 1631, is considered the first privately owned manufactory.

Since there were no free labor in the country, the state began to attribute, and later (1721) allowed to buy peasants to the factories. The assigned peasants had to work out their taxes to the state at a factory or a factory at certain rates. The state rendered assistance to owners of enterprises by land, forest, and money. The manufactories, founded with the support of the state, later received the name "pre-sessional" (from the Latin word "precession" - possession). To rebuild the country, the government needed a very large amount of money. For this, we had to restore the old taxes and introduce a number of new ones.

All estates were obliged to serve the state, and differed only in the nature of the obligations imposed on them. The population was divided into servicemen and people.

At the head of the service class stood about a hundred boyar families - the descendants of the former Great and appanage princes. They occupied senior positions in the military and civil administration, but during the 17th century, they were gradually crowded by people from the middle service classes. There was a merger of the boyars and nobles into one class of "public service people". According to its social and ethnic roots, it was distinguished by a marked diversity: initially, access to public service was open to all free people. As the state organization took shape, the service class became more and more closed.

The ability of noblemen to perform their military duties depended on the security of their estates with labor, on the transfer of peasants from one owner to another. In addition, the spontaneous mass migration of peasants to new lands (Ukraine, Wild Steppe, Siberia) led to disruptions in the tax system. Stabilization of the situation the government saw in the attachment of the peasants to the land, that is, in enslavement. Attaching to the land did not mean the enslavement of the peasants, they were still considered free men and could complain of oppressing the landowners in court. However, the landlords' power over the peasants gradually increased. More favorable was the position of state and palace peasants who did not submit to the landowners.

The rural peasant population consisted of two main categories. Peasants who lived on the lands of estates and estates, called the owner or privately owned. They carried a tax (a set of duties) in favor of the state and their feudal lord. The landowner received the right to speak in court for his peasants, he also had the right to a patrimonial trial of the population of his estate. The state reserved the right of court only for the most serious crimes. A place close to privately owned peasants was occupied by monastic peasants.

Another large category of the peasant population was the black-nosy peasantry. It lived on the outskirts of the country (Pomeranian North, the Urals, Siberia, the South), united in communities. Black-sowed peasants had no right to leave their lands if they did not find a change for themselves. They carried in favor of the state. Their position was easier than private ownership. "Black Earth" could sell, mortgage, pass by inheritance.

The middle position between the black-nosed and privately-owned peasants was occupied by the palace peasants, who served the economic needs of the royal court. They had self-government and obeyed the palace attendants.

Attaching to the other estates touched upon other classes; certain categories of the urban population were fixed on the ground. Nobles in Russia were no more free than peasants and citizens; they were bound by a lifetime service obligation. Each public group in the national structure was assigned a specific place. Applying flexible tactics, the central government was able to consolidate the Cossacks in the structure of the state. Moscow recognized for the Cossacks the right to self-government, to own land, provided them with food, money and weapons. The Cossacks, for their part, pledged to serve on the frontiers of the Moscow kingdom.

In the 17th century, the clergy was an influential estate, holding a monopoly in the sphere of education, culture, and ideology. The Orthodox understanding of class duties as a form of religious service led to the fact that the entire population carried general state duty: the nobles - personally, and the peasants and the townspeople - through taxes on the maintenance of troops. A peculiar system of Russian state serfdom is being created. The reign of Alexei Mikhailovich was amended in the judicial system. The Zemsky Sobor of 1649 developed a new code of laws, called the "Council Code". The most important areas of the Code were the protection of the interests of noblemen and citizens against the background of a certain restriction of the privileges of the boyars and clergy, as well as protectionism in favor of Russian merchants and industrialists. Peasants were legally attached to the ground.

Thus, the process of consolidation of estates takes place, their social framework is more clearly outlined. The dominant role belonged to the boyars and nobles. Regardless of the form of land ownership, they had to perform military service. There is a rapprochement between the social and political position of the nobility and the boyars. The difference between mansion and fiefdom is reduced to a minimum. A nobleman, even having sold or pledged the land to a monastery or a non-serving person, could bring it back. The nobles owned most of the peasant households (57% according to the census of 1678).

The position of the archers, gunners, state blacksmiths (so called "servicemen on the instrument") became more difficult. Their salaries decreased, many of the servicemen were transferred to the ranks of the townspeople and lost their former privileges (for example, the right to purchase land).

The number of townspeople - citizens - has grown. A significant part of the artisans worked for the state. Some craftsmen served the needs of the landowners (estate owners). According to the Council Code of 1649, only the townspeople could engage in craft and trade in the city. They entered the community and carried various duties, paid taxes, the totality of which was called a burden. The "best" people of the posad — merchants — led the townspeople, became deputies of the Zemsky Sobor, were in charge of collecting taxes and duties.

More closed became the peasant class. The social layers of slaves and "children" of the monastery disappeared. The legal order of privately-owned peasants was drawing closer to the position of state, black-nosed, who were increasingly seen as serfs.

As a result, by the middle of the XVII century, the ruin of times of unrest was overcome.

By the second half of the seventeenth century, the economic situation had changed. The state needed money. Raised taxes. The government of Tsar Alexei Mikhailovich increased indirect taxes, raising the price of salt 4 times in 1646. However, the increase in the tax on salt did not lead to the replenishment of the treasury, since the solvency of the population was undermined. Salt tax was abolished in 1647. It was decided to collect arrears for the last three years. In 1648, this resulted in an open rebellion in Moscow. The uprising in Moscow, called the "salt rebellion", was not the only one. For the twentieth anniversary (from 1630 to 1650), uprisings took place in 30 Russian cities: Veliky Ustyug, Novgorod, Voronezh, Kursk, Vladimir, Pskov, Siberian cities.

According to the modern historian AP Toroptsev, the state had no choice but to issue a copper coin in circulation. With this, the state wanted to save silver to pay salaries to the soldiers. This adversely affected the economy. Copper money merchants tried not to take for the goods. As a result, there was a depreciation of money. In addition, counterfeiters appeared in Moscow. This resulted in a whole series of grievances and uprisings. In the summer of 1662, for one silver ruble, eight copper coins were given. The government collected taxes in silver, while the population had to sell and buy products for copper money. The salary was also paid in copper money. The high cost of bread and other products that arose under these conditions led to hunger. Desperate, the Moscow people rose to revolt. Thus, by the middle of the 17th century, the state managed to overcome the consequences of the turmoil, but in the second half of the 17th century, tax increases, the grueling wars that Russia was leading, exhausted the treasury. To which the state adopted a series of measures that caused a series of popular discontent.

In the XVIII century. the development of Russia, as in the previous time, was carried out on a feudal serf basis. Feudal relations covered all spheres of public life, they spread to new territories and categories of the population, took more and more severe forms. However, the XVIII century. was a period when capitalist relations began to take shape in the depths of the feudal system, which in the process of the country's social and economic development was an event of exceptional importance. The new mode, being very weak, was strongly influenced by the ruling system and retained a number of features of serfdom.

Socio-economic development of Russia in the XVIII century. proceeded in difficult and contradictory conditions. At the heart of the population structure in the XVIII century. lay the principle of class. The Russian nobility became the dominant class. The class rights and privileges of the nobility, which consolidated its domination in economics and politics, were strengthened and expanded throughout the century. By the end of the XVIII century. nobles made up about 1% of the country's population. Certain privileges (exemption from the poll tax, recruitment, corporal punishment) were granted to the clergy and the Guild merchants, the so-called semi-privileged classes. The category of Guild merchants in the population was only 0.5%. By the end of the century, a semi-privileged military-service class (Cossacks, Kalmyks, part of the Bashkirs) was formed, which constituted less than 2% of the total population. It was exempted from the head tax, the recruitment duty, but it carried obligatory military service on special conditions. The bulk of the population of the country were tax-paying classes (peasants, burghers, craft artisans). By the end of the century, the taxed population of cities accounted for just over 3% of the total population. Over 90% of the population were peasants who were divided into two broad categories: state and landowners. Peasants of all categories were serfs. They were attached to the land, they paid feudal rent, carried recruitment duties, and experienced all the lack of rights in the class. The most difficult was the situation of privately-owned peasants who were in the unlimited power and property of the landlords. In the non-chernozem zone, in conditions of infertile soils, about 55% of the landowners' peasants were transferred to monetary rent, which was often supplemented with real money. Its size is growing rapidly. The rents, according to specialists, from 1713 to 1753 increased from 30 rubles to 200. Much of it was paid by the peasants through the sale of their handicrafts and non-agricultural products in the market, as well as from money received from various jobs in cities and on manufactories. All this testified to the destruction of the natural economy of the village, to the strengthening of relations of the obscene farm with the market. In the non-chernozem zone, areas appeared, residents of villages and villages that specialized in various non-agricultural industries: leather production (Kimry of the Tver province), weaving (Ivanovo-Vladimir province), metal working (Lyskovo, Pavlovo, Murashkino of the Nizhny Novgorod province). Handicraft production gradually grew into a manufactory here. In the chernozem part of the country, mining rent was widely practiced, sometimes reaching 4-5 days a week. The growth of corvee was accompanied by a sharp increase in the size of the lordly plowing due to the reduction of peasant holdings. The landowners took plots from a part of the peasants and transferred them to a month. Such peasants, as a rule, did not have their own farms and worked almost the entire week on the lordly plowing, receiving meager monthly maintenance. They did not have time to practice a craft, trade. The landowner was not associated with the market in this zone. And the relationship of landlords with the market strengthened.

Due to the high scale of the Urals production at that time, Russia by the middle of the century smelted 2 million pounds of pig iron, one and a half times more than the advanced England in those times. At the beginning of the century, Russia imported iron from abroad, and in the middle of the century, soft, malleable Ural iron became one of the important goods of Russian export. After ferrous metallurgy non-ferrous has developed. The weapon industry and shipbuilding received a powerful push in its development. The major centers of light industry were Moscow and St. Petersburg. Linen, cloth, sailing, leather manufactories originated in the central regions of Russia. The number of cities also grew rapidly. In the Moscow provinces formed the largest industrial region of the country. Moscow, Tula, Yaroslavl, Vladimir, Kaluga possessed a developed and diversified manufacture. The expansion of internal volume led to a deepening of specialization in the production of goods and products of every kind, which in turn caused the further development of the All-Russian market. At the end of the century, over 1,600 trade fairs were drawn into domestic trade.

The peculiarity of the foreign trade of Russia in the XVIII century. there was a significant predominance of exports over imports. The main exported goods were flax, hemp, wood, leather, canvas, canvas, bread. In the second half of the century, iron exports rose sharply. All this testified to the increasing role of commodity-money relations and the manufacturing industry in the country's economy (Avanesova, 2015).

Thus, in this large and important historical period, quite contradictory circumstances were formed in Russia, which were characterized by the fact that feudal relations delayed and slowed the growth of capitalist relations, but they could not stop their objective development.

CONCLUSION

Social and economic factors of development of the Russian public power. The origin, formation and further development of Russian statehood (in the context of the topic under consideration) is the emergence and development of the Russian state, its various types, forms and functions at various stages of Russian history, continuity and renewal of the political, structural and territorial organization of Russian society, i.e.. state-legal processes occurring over a long period of life of the Russian ethnos.

We can distinguish the following specific laws of the evolution of Russian statehood. Specific issues for the Russian statehood, which are solved in the centuries-old history of Russia and have, in turn, a decisive influence on its statehood, give this statehood an identity that is worthy of theoretical understanding:

1. The peasant question (the question of liberating the peasants and allotting them land);
2. The national question (the question of the sovereignty and rights of peoples within Russia);
3. The geopolitical issue (the question of relations with countries - "closest neighbors", as well as distant countries);
4. The question of the modernization of Russia (the problem of choosing the historical and socio-economic path of development) (Lubsky, R. A., 2015).

The peasant question is the question of how to most effectively combine the farmer, the peasant with the land, taking into account the spatial and climatic conditions of Russia, traditions and the psychology of the people. These are attempts of the state to create and consolidate the most profitable way of farming on the land for farmers and society.

In the history of Russian statehood, all the time has gone and there is a search for such most effective forms focused on the key features of the economic structure. Individual-family farming, household-family cooperation and organization of agricultural labor, individual farming, farming, communal, communal-serf, kolkhoz and sovkhoz economic activity - all these methods are tested by the state for several centuries.

The national question also arises in the depth of the centuries in the process of the formation of the Russian state by three ethnic groups: Slavic, Finno-Ugric, Turkic, with the dominant role of the Slavic ethnic group and in certain areas of its Russian basis.

Attempts to solve the national question have been characterized for centuries by different processes: here both violent and voluntary forms of joining of certain nationalities to the population of the Russian state, invasive and defensive wars, peaceful and violent forms of resolving ethnic conflicts, seizures in the Russian state by other ethnic groups, their appearance in key government positions, sometimes hectic, but mostly peaceful, friendly e state and the coexistence of ethnic groups.

Over the centuries, in the history of Russian statehood, various ethnic economic structures, religious systems collide: mainly Orthodox Christian and Muslim, national psychologies, legal systems, cultural values and everyday characteristics - all this is "digested" in a huge historical cauldron in a huge Eurasian space.

Closely related to the national geopolitical issue. It covers the problems and processes of reunification with Russia of other states, accession to the population of Russia, including by force, and the separation of its peoples and their state entities. It includes this issue and the problem of protecting reunited or acquired territories, protecting borders, moving over the centuries of the Slavic ethnos to the maritime borders, taking into account and observing the geopolitical interests of Russia by other states.

Geopolitics is currently acquiring the status of an important part of the theory of the state. As a politician, it is also a constant, general social function of the Russian statehood, which has become especially significant since the XVIth century. The constancy of this function has manifested itself over the centuries: repeated divisions of Poland, wars for access to the Baltic and

Black Seas, colonization of Siberia, the problem of the southern borders protecting the state from Muslim fundamentalism, the problem of including the entire Volga as a single waterway into the territorial expanses of Russia, the problem of the Kuril Islands - all this and much more filled the bright pages of the table in which the "eternal" geopolitical interests of the Russian statehood are historically listed.

Modernization is a capacious and extensive process aimed at ensuring that the quality of life of Russian society, the state and characteristics of the socio-economic structure, the human condition, the state-legal organization of society and the activities of the institutions of statehood, in general, raise the whole life to world standards the possibility to apply the "human dimension" in the social assessment of the very existence of the Russian ethnos.

Modernization is a capacious and extensive process aimed at ensuring that the quality of life of Russian society, the state and characteristics of the socio-economic structure, the human condition, the state-legal organization of society and the activities of the institutions of statehood, in general, raise the whole life to world standards the possibility to apply the "human dimension" in the social assessment of the very existence of the Russian ethnos. And this process has also been for more than three hundred years (it should be read from Peter the Great - it is from the seventeenth century that it begins to be traced most clearly) powerfully fills the content of another general social function of Russian statehood, is another "eternal" issue of the active side of the Russian state (Omelchenko N.A., 2013).

The movement towards a social state of law, the formation and maintenance of human rights and freedoms, a breakthrough in the spiritual life - the flourishing of personality, creative, independent individualism, enterprise (instead of social dependency, equalization) - all this and many other very important areas of modernization. But they do not affect all the vital activity of a society, but rather individual social institutions, including the institutions of statehood. And in this movement, modernization eliminates faults, gaps between the state of a particular society and the world's most effective models, standards of living.

The main factors determining the development of Russia in various periods of the country's history - from ancient times to the present day. Historical factors are understood as those or other circumstances that have an objective impact - positive or negative - on the welfare of the people and the state.

For the first time, historian Vasily Osipovich Klyuchevsky consistently applied factor analysis in Russian historiography, thanks to which he was able to create perhaps the best description of the history of Ancient and Muscovite

Russia in terms of explaining the causes of historical processes. However, his course in the history of Russia covers only the period until the middle of the 19th century, and Kliuchevskii's liberal views and critical attitude to the Romanov dynasty markedly reflected on his presentation of Russian history of the 17th – 19th centuries, which Klyuchevskii's is relatively biased. Klyuchevskiy conducted a brilliant analysis of the natural-geographical and internal factors of the history of Russia, but the foreign policy and military factors of the history of Russia diverted much less attention.

The main groups of factors include:

1. **Natural Factors:** Geographical features of the country's territory or of newly joined lands (climate, relief, availability of rivers and seas, availability of available resources).
2. **Political Factors:**
    a. *Foreign Policy Factors:* The situation in neighboring countries and the nature of relations with them.
    b. *Internal Political (Social) Factors:* The political and spiritual state of the elite and the people, the established system of social relations, internal social contradictions and social conflicts.
3. **Economic Factors:**
    a. *External Economic Factors:* Proximity or remoteness from trade routes, qualitative and quantitative composition of the export and import of the country.
    b. *Internal Economic Factors:* The achieved material state of society, the availability of natural resources and their involvement in the economy, the availability of transport and production infrastructure and its development, economic crises.
4. **Technological, scientific, educational and cultural factors:** the development and borrowing of new technologies, important for the state of the whole society, trends in the fields of science, education, art and culture.
5. **Military Factors:** The level of combat capability of the army, military victories and defeats and related gains or losses (Ponomareva E.G., 2013).

Among the political factors proper is, firstly, the hypertrophied role of the state, authoritarianism, the predominance of the administrative-bureaucratic model of management, the state is built on the basis of top-down management, as well as the system of relations between the government and society (according to the principle "I am the head, you are a fool "), policeman, the power apparatus, and personalism, the role of the individual in the system of state and municipal government (as a god per capita puts to the ruler). In addition, there is disrespect for the law, law, a weak role of civil institutions and a low political culture. To a certain extent, low political culture and defective sense of justice determine everything else. The yoke, serfdom, autocracy, the complete lack of rights of the individual are the reasons for the low political culture in the society of that time.

All these social, political, economic factors of the development of the Russian statehood operated on the territory of Russia from the Xth to the beginning of the XIXth centuries, and some of them still exist today.

REFERENCES

Avanesova, N. G., & Muravskaya, E. A. (2015). On the formation of the modern Russian statehood. *Scientific-Methodical Electronic Journal "Concept", 14,* 16-20. Retrieved from http://e-koncept.ru/2015/95135.htm (in Russian)

Dmitriev, Y. A. (2005). The concept and main factors determining the development of the Russian state. *Problems of the Theory of State and Law.* Retrieved from https://law.wikireading.ru/7192 (in Russian)

Factors of Russian History. (n.d.). Retrieved from https://ruxpert.ru/Factors_history_Russia (in Russian)

Historical features of the formation and development of Russian statehood. In *Modern Political Extremism.* Moscow: ROSPEN, 2009. Retrieved from http://www.ekstremizm.ru/biblioteka/knigi/item/246-formirovanie-i-razvitie-rossiyskoy-gosudarstvennosti (in Russian)

Komarov, A. V., & Muraveva, L. A. (2018). Formation of the Russian statehood: main features and features. *Science. Society. Defense, 4*(17). Retrieved from https://cyberleninka.ru/article/n/stanovlenie-rossiyskoy-gosudarstvennosti-osnovnye-cherty-i-osobennosti (in Russian)

Lubsky, R. A. (2015). *Russian statehood as a social reality: dissertation.* Retrieved from http://cheloveknauka.com/rossiyskaya-gosudarstvennost-kak-sotsialnaya-realnost (in Russian)

Omelchenko, N. A. (2013). On the concept of "Statehood", traditional foundations, conditions and factors of the formation of the Russian statehood. *Bulletin of the State University of Management, 20.* Retrieved from https://cyberleninka.ru/article/n/o-ponyatii-gosudarstvennost-traditsionnyh-osnovah-usloviyah-i-faktorah-formirovaniya-rossiyskoy-gosudarstvennosti (in Russian)

Ponomareva, E. G. (2013). *Internal and external factors of development of the Russian statehood. Russian statehood: historical traditions and challenges of the XXI century*. Materials of the All-Russian Scientific and Public Conference, Sept. 19, 2012, V. Novgorod. Retrieved from https://mgimo.ru/upload/iblock/76d/76d880612459a1bf442dcd0dba94e23b.pdf (in Russian)

Chapter 3
Socio-Economic Situation in Russia in the 19th-Early 20th Centuries

Bogdan Ershov
Voronezh State Technical University, Russia

ABSTRACT

This chapter discusses the processes of capitalization of Russia in the 19th century. It is shown that during the period of imperialism, quantitative and qualitative changes occurred in the composition and position of the Russian bourgeoisie. The economic face of the Russian bourgeoisie, as well as the bourgeoisie of other developed capitalist countries, revealed the most advanced forms of capital organization. But the structure of the upper strata of the Russian bourgeoisie was different from the Western European segment. Before the First World War, two types of Russian capitalists were distinguished, both in origin and in the form of exploitation and organization of capital. During the period of imperialism, Moscow gradually became monopolistic. The Moscow capitalist elite has not yet become a financial oligarchy, it has not created large corporations, and financial and industrial groups.

DOI: 10.4018/978-1-5225-9985-2.ch003

INTRODUCTION

The modern period of development of all spheres of life of the Russian state - economic, social, political, cultural - is characterized by active efforts to transform the institutional environment. However, the results of the reforms of the last decade do not correspond to the expected expectations.

The past market reforms radically changed the country's economic potential, Russia's position in the international arena, and destabilized its social climate. Market reforms were accompanied by a decrease in the efficiency of the national economy, a sharp decline in production volumes, a decrease in the level and quality of life of the population, environmental degradation, that is, a sharp degradation of the political and socio-economic situation in the country.

This situation has caused and sharpened attention as a general, the study of the features of the economic system and economic development of Russia and, as a particular, the analysis of the reasons that contributed to the failure of institutional reforms that accompanied the reform processes in Russia. Discussions about the further development of the country are becoming more intense. Should Russia use the Western European or East Asian model, is it possible to transform the foreign institutional structures into Russian soil without any pain?

Any model of development of the national economy is not only a peculiar combination of internal and external factors determined by national or geopolitical features, but also has specific features related to different historical stages and associated with the basic conditions at each of them. Therefore, in the process of any reforms, the key issue is the issue of the compliance of the chosen model of economic development and the institutions adequate to it to the national traditional institutional forms developed over the centuries, among which the national economic mentality is one of the main ones. That is, it is a question about the relationship between the traditions of society and the processes of renewal.

Scientifically, the problems of opportunities and ways of transforming and implanting economic institutions, and, most importantly, their consequences, are under development. Ignoring the factors influencing these processes, among which one of the important places is occupied by the national mentality, leads to the strengthening of economic and social imbalances, to the many negative consequences that are observed in Russian reality. The aim of the study is to analyze the current stage of the reform of the Russian socio-economic system;

determination of the dependence of the results of the reformation processes in the history of Russia, consisting in transplantation into the socio-economic sphere of foreign institutional forms, on their compliance with traditional informal institutions, first of all, the economic mentality that influences the choice and formation of the type of economic system that has a narrow national identity; determining the characteristics of the national economic mentality, which is based on tradition as a component of the institutional environment, based on the study and evaluation of its natural and institutional factors.

The theoretical and methodological basis of the chapters of the book are the works of modern foreign and domestic scientists - both economists and sociologists - specialists in the theory of the economic development of Russia.

In developing this problem, the following research methods were used: the study of scientific and methodical literature, dialectical cognition and institutional analysis. The range of tasks to be analyzed determined the need to use appropriate methodological tools, namely, civilizational, historical and institutional approaches. The informational basis of the study was domestic and foreign monographic and periodicals. The book takes into account the most important provisions of the theory of modernization, especially concerning the demographic and social problems of the formation of Russian cities as industrial centers, which are among the important processes of transition from an agrarian society to an industrial one.

The study used the method of analysis and processing of documentary data, which allowed to identify the total and particular in the study period. A comparative historical approach to the characterization of the socio-economic situation in Russia made it possible to identify objective regularities of demographic processes. Problem-chronological method allowed us to trace the dynamics of the studied socio-economic phenomena. Based on the statistical method, quantitative indicators of the formation of the urban population and the economy of urban centers, the budgetary capacity of cities and the urban economy are analyzed.

The study used various approaches, methods, conceptual apparatus and theoretical concepts used in disciplines related to history, primarily historical geography, demography, sociology and economics. The use of these methods: allowed to deeper consider the general and specific features of the socio-economic development of the country, the holistic nature of the provincial cities. In book undertook a comprehensive study of the state of industry and agricultural production in Russia during the period of capitalist transformations in the XIX - early XX centuries. Some documents of personal origin are used in the work, mainly memoirs of Russian political figures related to the modernization of the country. Data from this category of sources was used primarily to compare them with the estimates of the tsarist economic policy.

The practical significance of the monograph is the possibility of using the findings to create works on the economic history of Russia. Identifying the positive and negative aspects of the Russian economy is of practical importance, since it can serve as a guide when choosing the main directions of its further development.

THE POSITION OF DIFFERENT CLASSES OF RUSSIAN SOCIETY

By the end of the 19th and the beginning of the 20th century, the Russian Empire was the largest territorial state in the world. The country stretched from the Baltic Sea to the Pacific Ocean and from the Arctic Ocean to the deserts of Central Asia. Her nature was extremely varied. The economic development of various regions of the country remained uneven, especially developing industrial regions stood out: Moscow, St. Petersburg, Riga, Lodz, South Russian, and the Urals. The intensive development of Siberia and the Far East began, where Krasnoyarsk, Novonikolaevsk and Vladivostok became centers. However, the huge spaces were extremely weakly connected with each other by transport arteries.

In most of the developed regions of the Russian Empire, agricultural production predominated. In the central regions of the European part of the country there was a tendency to agrarian overpopulation, which led to a shortage of land. At the same time, the population density beyond the Urals did not exceed 1 person / km 2.

In 1897 the first population census was conducted in Russia. It was over 125 million people. Population growth was rapid. In 1860 the population was 75 million people. Of these: 14 million - the urban population, the rest - rural.

The reforms of the 1860s and 1870s opened new prospects for Russia, creating an opportunity for broad development of market relations. The country embarked on the path of capitalist development.

The last Romanov was Nicholas II (1894 - 1917). In the first months of his reign, the young emperor expressed his intention with particular force to follow his father's system in the internal administration of the state and promised "to guard the beginning of the autocracy as firmly and unswervingly," as Alexander III guarded him.

Russia was a multiethnic state in which lived more than a hundred different large nationalities and small national groups. On socio-economic development, they stood on a different level - from the most primitive forms of the patriarchal-tribal system and the nomadic hunting-cattle farm to developed capitalist relations (Acceleration, 1984).

The interweaving of advanced capitalist forms of economy with pre-capitalist and patriarchal forms reflected on the social structure of the population. Although the city played a leading role in the social and economic life, the rural population greatly prevailed over the urban population. The prosperous rural masters were more than the small capitalists in the city. Together they made up a significant stratum of the country's population.

In the early twentieth century. there were noticeable changes in the quantitative composition of the main social groups of capitalist Russia. In 1,5 times increased in comparison with the data for the XIX century. the number of workers increased by almost 40%, and the number of small capitalists increased, and by 1/3 - the proletarianized and pauperized peasants. However, the social processes noted were slow, as indicated by insignificant changes in the relative weight of each of these groups.

In the years 1900 - 1913. significant changes took place in the structure and quantity of the working class. The total number of the working class in 1913 was 17.8 million. The proportion of workers in the most technically equipped branches of industry increased significantly: in machine building, metallurgy, and also in railways. In large cities, the number and proportion of the industrial proletariat increased. Powerful capitalist enterprises united and rallied the workers into large proletarian collectives. At these enterprises, there were significant cadres of permanent hereditary workers who forever broke the connection with the land. The number of hereditary workers in 1913 was more than half of the entire working class. In the 1900s, the proportion of female workers increased significantly: in some industries, they accounted for one-third of all workers, and in the textile industry, more than half. Child labor was widely used (Anap'ich, 1991).

The concentration of workers in the largest industrial enterprises has increased considerably. The highest level it reached in the cotton and metallurgical industries. Somewhat lower, she was in the engineering, mining and sugar industries. The concentration of workers at the largest industrial enterprises and in industrial centers rallied the multinational units of the Russian proletariat into a single international force. This unity was strengthened in the general revolutionary cash struggle. The growth of the cash consciousness of the proletariat was also promoted by the increased cultural level of the workers-among the industrial workers there was a higher literacy rate.

As a result of the conquests of the revolution of 1905-1907. workers have achieved a significant increase in wages. However, in connection with the growth of prices for consumer goods, the real salary was very low.

The working conditions at the enterprises even in the most developed branches of industry remained heavy. There was still a high working day. Almost all enterprises did not have any labor protection. Occupational diseases and injuries were common. Continued to remain a low level of medical care. Housing conditions, as before, were very difficult.

Significantly changing the social and economic appearance of the village. The peasantry with its economy lost the features inherent in it as a class of the old feudal society. The process of social and economic differentiation of the peasantry in the Russian village had its own peculiarities: the rural population, despite the increasing withdrawal of peasants to cities and industrial centers, continued to grow and remained the most numerous class in the population structure.

The peculiarity of the relations between the new classes that emerged in the countryside-the kulaks and the poor strata of the peasantry-was that the kulaks preferred to profit, not by investing capital in agricultural production, but by means of usury and bonded trade.

Despite the progressive nature of capitalization processes, the withdrawal of a considerable mass of peasants into industry, their conversion into wage workers, agrarian overpopulation during the period of imperialism has increased. Although during the revolution of 1905 - 1907 gg. the peasantry's performances were brutally suppressed, the hopelessness of the situation of the landless and defenched peasantry with new force pushed him into the struggle. During the period of imperialism, there are quantitative and qualitative changes in the composition and position of the Russian bourgeoisie.

The economic face of the Russian bourgeoisie, like the bourgeoisie of other, capitalistically developed countries, determined the most advanced forms of capital organization. But the structure of the upper strata of the Russian bourgeoisie differed from the West European number of features. Before the First World War, two types of Russian capitalists are distinguished, both in their origin and in the form of exploitation and organization of capital. Even in the period of pre-monopoly capitalism, there was a big bourgeoisie in the leading industrial centers, which transformed its family firms into joint-stock companies with a narrow circle of owners of large units. In this group of the bourgeoisie, mainly provincial, Moscow capitalists stand out, claiming the role of spokesmen for the interests of Russian commercial and industrial circles. In the period of imperialism, Moscow's large capital is gradually becoming monopolistic. Moscow capitalist elite has not yet turned into a financial oligarchy, has not created major concerns, financial and industrial groups. But she did not miss her leadership in the Russian commercial and industrial circles.

Another type of large Russian capitalist represented a narrow layer of financial oligarchy, mostly St. Petersburg, which came not from hereditary entrepreneurs, but from among the top employees of banking and industrial monopolies. Among them, former senior officials of the Ministry of Finance, the State Bank and other state institutions prevailed. They controlled the huge capitals of joint-stock industrial and financial enterprises (Avrekh, 1966).

In addition, there was another large group of capitalists, mostly provincial, which operated mainly in the sphere of commercial capital. In the period of imperialism, the multinational character of the Russian bourgeoisie is further strengthened: it included a large group of capitalists of foreign origin and national margins.

Simultaneously with the process of folding the system of monopoly capital, the process of political consolidation of the bourgeoisie also took place. It sought to expand its importance in the political life of the country and in the affairs of the autocratic state.

The political consolidation of the bourgeoisie took place in the conditions of an acute struggle against the proletariat. Under the influence of this factor, the first political parties of the bourgeoisie that arose during the first Russian revolution came out with counter-revolutionary programs. However, the Russian bourgeoisie did not create a strong own political party. In the struggle against the revolution, the Russian bourgeoisie united with the nobility, which retained its political dominance.

In the hands of the local nobility there was a huge land fund, the value of which was 60% higher than the total mass of the share capital in the country. During the period of imperialism, the largest landed estates lost their purely noble character.

Despite the fact that the large local gentry was a minority among the propertied upper classes, it occupied a dominant position at all levels of state administration. The first popular revolution forced the local nobility to create political parties and organizations. These parties were united by the Council of the United Nobility, created in 1906, which began to define basically the policy of the government.

The nobility supplied the cadres of the supreme bureaucracy, which exercised supreme authority on the ground. At the same time, it gradually replenished from other classes, which gave it a bourgeois character. This determined the duality of the social person of the Russian bureaucracy. Although most of the higher civilian and military ranks were made up of hereditary noblemen, the bureaucracy, expressing the interests of the nobility, gradually became closer to the financial and industrial world. There were stable links between the state apparatus and the financial elite of monopoly capital. In the early twentieth century. Russia in the economic sense has reached an average level of development in comparison with the advanced capitalist states and in it all basic contradictions characteristic for the newest stage of development of capitalism - imperialism were shown.

The retention of feudal remnants in the economy and the socio-political system of the Russian state in the form of military-feudal imperialism slowed and slowed down the pace of economic development, but at the same time intensified and exacerbated the social and political contradictions of Russian imperialism. Conditions were created for strengthening the unity of the entire working people of Russia in the struggle against the autocracy, for democratic reconstruction and for socialism.

In March 1902, an agreement was signed between Russia and China on the phased withdrawal of troops from Manchuria, where they were in 1902 after participating in suppressing the uprising of theirs. The first stage of the evacuation was carried out exactly on time, and then in Petersburg there were fears that, following the withdrawal of Russian troops, Manchuria would fall into the hands of Japan or some other power. China was demanded of the corresponding guarantees, but the Chinese government replied that it would conduct further negotiations on Manchuria only after the withdrawal of the Russian troops. The dispute was intervened by Britain, the United States and Japan, which protested to St. Petersburg in connection with the delay in the implementation of the agreement. Japanese diplomacy was particularly active (Balakina, 2000).

Negotiations between Russia and Japan were not successful. The Russian-Japanese war was mainly caused by rivalry between Russia and Japan in the sphere of influence in China and Korea. Japan in the course of negotiations increasingly tightened its position. Russia was making concessions. But in the autumn of 1903, Russian warships were sent to the Korean port of Chemulpo to guard the diplomatic mission, and Russian troops did not leave Manchuria on the due date. This caused an outburst of outrage in Japan (although there were ships of other countries in Chemulpo).

THE CAUSES AND CONSEQUENCES OF THE RUSSIAN-JAPANESE WAR

The war began on January 26, 1904, in the context of Russia's foreign policy isolation. The Japanese fleet blocked the cruiser Varyag and the gunboat Koreyets in Chemulpo. They made a heroic but unsuccessful attempt at a breakthrough. After this, the team went ashore, the Varyag was flooded, and the Korean was blown up. On the night of January 27, Japanese destroyers attacked a Russian squadron on the roadstead of Port Arthur, and damaged two battleships and one cruiser.

Militarily, Russia was stronger than Japan. But the bulk of her armed forces were far from the theater of military operations. On the Trans-Siberian Railway, which was not completely completed yet, no more than two divisions a month arrived. In addition, throughout the war, Britain and the United States generously helped Japan with loans, coal, oil, strategic raw materials and armaments. On the English shipyards, ships were built for Japan.

Trying to accumulate reserves, the Russian command at the beginning of the war acted extremely passively. At the head of the Manchurian army, General A. N. Kuropatkin. He was an experienced military leader, but he was not very determined. On the contrary, the Japanese command acted quickly and aggressively.

February - March, the Japanese army landed and deployed in Korea, and in April, breaking through the Russian defense, invaded Manchuria. Soon around Port-Arthur, the siege ring began to shrink.

On August 6, 1904, the first storm of Port Arthur began. But he completely failed, and the Japanese had to move to a long siege of the fortress, concentrating considerable military forces at Port Arthur. The siege of the fortress lasted almost eight months. But the general strategic situation on other sectors of the front by this time was clearly not in favor of the Russian troops. And December 20, 1904, the commandant of the fortress, AM. Stessel passed Port Arthur to the Japanese. This was the first noticeably sensitive blow to Russia's prestige (Belova, 1991).

But his tragic end began as early as June 1904, when the Japanese massively moved to the north. Kuropatkin again showed slowness in the actions and gave the Japanese the opportunity to fully mobilize their armies in their chosen strategic direction. He moved against the Japanese corps in 30 thousand people under the command of General Stackelberg. In the battle of Wafangow in June 1904, the frontal attack of the Japanese was repulsed, but the Russian command failed to develop the initial success, and gave the order to retreat. Wafangou is a city and station of the CER, only 150 versts north of Port Arthur. And the guilty defeat was, first of all, Kuropatkin himself, who with an easy heart ordered to advance and did not feel remorse, ordering him to retreat.

On August 17 - 21 a major Laoliang battle took place, which was marked by special bloodshed. And again Kuropatkin, fearing for his rear communications, failed to organize a counteroffensive and, thereby, again missed the real chances to win. Russian troops retreated even further to the north of Manchuria, to Mukden.

In September, receiving finally the long-awaited reinforcements, Kuropatkin decided to organize an offensive. But for victory, a clear, coordinated organization of the offensive is also needed. But the plan was, to put it mildly, developed unsuccessfully. They decided to advance through the mountainous terrain, lacking the mountain tools, and the cavalry, which at that time was the most maneuverable part of the troops, could not fully use their fighting qualities in these conditions. Just fearing the flanking blows of the Japanese, Kuropatkin left a significant portion of the forces in reserve.

The Japanese from September 22 to October 4, 1904, also decided to launch offensive operations near the Shah River. Russian troops, conducted military operations sluggishly, missed the possibility of reaching the right flank of the enemy, which would significantly affect the successful outcome of the battle. The Japanese moved into a counter-offensive in the center and on the left flank of the Russian troops. Their fighting was much more successful. And our commander-in-chief did not believe in victory and gave the order to retreat. As a result, having lost more than 40 thousand people without the benefit to the cause, the Russian troops withdrew and occupied a new line of defense. The Japanese, although they won in this battle, were extremely exhausted, did not try to pursue the departing and also went to the deaf defense.

Taking advantage of the respite provided in the battles, Kuropatkin at the end of October 1904 divided the Russian troops into three armies under his general guidance. And on January 25 - 28, 1905, an attempt was made by the forces of the main second army with a strategic task to cover the left flank of the Japanese front. The most stubborn battles took place around the village of Sandepu. But the offensive was poorly organized, there was a shortage of forces attacking, there was obvious fatigue. The offensive did not give a positive result. And on the night of 18 to 19 February 1905, the Japanese army itself went into a counter-offensive.

The Mukden battle began, which lasted until February 25. And although the forces of the Russian troops were superior to the Japanese, Russian forces could not win victories in the battle. The Japanese plan consisted in the girth of both flanks of the Russian army. The unsuccessful maneuvering of the Russian troops allowed the Japanese troops to break the front east of Mukden, as a result of which the right wing of the Russian troops was in a difficult situation. The troops were almost in a semi-circle. Only the heroic fortitude of certain parts of the Russian army, and even the lack of strength of the Japanese, allowed the main forces to get out of the encirclement with great losses.

As a result of the entire land company, Japan was able to retain almost the entire southern part of Manchuria.

After Mukden's battle, General Kuropatkin was succeeded by N.Linevich. But by that time none of the belligerents was physically able to conduct active combat operations (Bovykin, 1959).

May 27, 1905, the Tsushima battle began, in which our troops also suffered defeat. The Japanese had a stronger weapon than the Russians, and the forces were not equal. The goal of this battle was to break through to Vladivostok and ensure domination not only in the battle area, but throughout the Sea of Japan. But only 1 cruiser and 2 destroyers managed to break through to Vladivostok.

After Mukden in the land theater of active hostilities was practically not carried out. Both opposing sides were exhausted by this time both morally and materially. Especially it was felt by the Japanese.

In Japan, much earlier than in Russia, understood the hopelessness of the planned enterprise. Through side channels of diplomacy, Russian Minister Witte was invited to meet with Japanese representatives and begin negotiations on peace. Immediately after the Battle of Tsushima, Japan asked the United States to mediate peace. The Russian autocracy, intimidated by the impending revolution and general discontent in the country by the results of the Far Eastern company, agreed to sit down at the negotiating table. Negotiations were like in the American city of Portsmouth. On September 5, 1905, the Portsmouth Peace Treaty was signed between Russia and Japan. Under this agreement, the Russian government ceded Japan to the southern part of Sakhalin Island and renounced the right to lease the Kwantung Peninsula with Port Arthur and the South Manchurian Railway. Similarly, the Russian government recognized the "special" interests of Japan in Korea. The signing of such a treaty did not bring the victorious laurels to the Russian state and did not raise its prestige in the world.

In 1905-1907 years Stolypin's agrarian reform was carried out. The main goal was to enlist the support of the broad strata of the peasantry and prevent a new agrarian war. In carrying out the reform, the government did not seek to affect the interests of the landlords. In the post-reform period and in the early 20th century. the government could not protect the aristocratic landownership from the reduction, but the large and small local nobility continued to constitute the most reliable support of the autocracy. Push it would be for the regime to commit suicide (Ershov, 2012).

In addition, the nobility class organizations, including the council of the united nobility, had a great influence on Nicholas II and his entourage. The members of the government, let alone the prime minister, who raised the issue of the alienation of the landed estates, could not stay in his place, let alone organize such a reform. The reformers also took into account the fact that landlord farms produced a substantial part of marketable grain. Another goal was the destruction of the rural community in the struggle of 1905-1907, the reformers understood that the main thing in the peasant movement was the question of land, and did not seek to immediately destroy the administrative organization of the community (Ershov, 2013).

CONCLUSION

Thus, in the 19th century, Russia's socio-economic goals were closely linked to socio-political goals. It was planned to abolish the land community, its economic mechanism of land distribution, on the one hand, which was the basis of the social unity of the community, and on the other hand, it held back the development of agricultural technology. The ultimate economic goal of the reforms should be the general increase in the country's agriculture, the transformation of the agrarian sector into the economic base of the new Russia.

REFERENCES

Acceleration, V. N. (1984). Modern American bourgeois historiography about the socio-economic development of Siberia in the era of capitalism. *Questions of the socio-economic development of Siberia in the period of capitalism,* 194-206.

Anap'ich, B. V., & Ganelin, R. S. (1991). The crisis of power in Russia: reforms and the revolutionary process. *1905 and 1917 History of the USSR, 2,* 96-106.

Avrekh, A. Y. (1966). Tsarism and the Third June system. Academic Press.

Balakina, T. I. (2000). *World Art. Russia IX - beg. XX century*. Academic Press. (in Russian)

Belova, T. (1991). *Culture and power*. Academic Press. (in Russian)

Bovykin, V.I. (1959) Banks and military industry of Russia on the eve of the First World War. *Historical Notes, 64*, 82-135.

Bovykin, V. I., & Laverychev, V. Y. (1981). Socio-economic and political background of the Great October Socialist Revolution. *Soviet historiography of the Great October Socialist Revolution,* 27-55.

Culture of the post-war decade - Russia. (n.d.). Retrieved from http://russia.rin.ru/guides/7170.html (in Russian)

Culture: Theories and problems. (1995). Academic Press. (in Russian)

Dorogova, L. N. (n.d.). Soviet Culture and Modern Russia. *Culturology.* Retrieved from http://web-local.rudn.ru/web-local/uem/ido/1/cult/cu3-7.html (in Russian)

Dorogova, L. N., Pykhanov, Y. V., & Mareeva, E. V. (n.d.). *Culturology: Electronic textbook*. Retrieved from http://ido.rudn.ru/ffec/cult-index.html (in Russian)

Dracha, G. V. (2000). *Culturology*. Academic Press. (in Russian)

Dubrovsky, S. M. (1975). *Agriculture and peasantry of Russia in the period of imperialism.*

Ershov, B. A. (2012). *The Russian Orthodox Church in the system of public relations in the XIX– early XX centuries* (PhD dissertation). Kursk State University. (in Russian)

Ershov, B. A. (2012). Historiographical aspects of the relationship between the Russian Orthodox Church and state structures in the provinces of the Central Chernozem region in the XIX -early XX centuries. *Bulletin of the Voronezh State Technical University. Series Humanities, 8(11),* 188–192. (in Russian)

Ershov, B.A. (2012). State legal regulation of the activities of the Russian Orthodox Church in the provinces of the Central Chernozem region in the XIX -early XX centuries. *Historical, philosophical, political and legal sciences, culturology and arthistory. Questions of theory and practice,* 75-78.

Ershov, B. A. (2013). Russian Orthodox Church in the structure of public administration in the XIX -early XX centuries: Monograph. Voronezh State Technical University.

Chapter 4
Revolutionary Upheavals in Russia in the Early 20th Century

Bogdan Ershov
Voronezh State Technical University, Russia

ABSTRACT

This chapter examines the social contradictions and the inability of the government to solve the main political problems that led to the deep socio-political crisis of Russia in the early 20th century. This was expressed in the struggle of the workers against the autocratic police system, in the creation of radical, left-wing political parties and liberal opposition unions, in disputes within the ruling elite, and fluctuations in the government's course. All these sociopolitical contradictions and problems were aggravated in the conditions of the deep economic crisis that Russia, like all other European powers, experienced in the early 20th century. Particular attention is drawn to the fact that in the late 19th to early 20th centuries in Russia, as in other capitalist countries, monopolistic associations in industry, commerce, and transport became widespread.

INTRODUCTION

The change in the form of ownership of peasant land, the transformation of peasants into full-fledged owners of their allotments was assumed by the law of 1910. first of all, by "strengthening" allotments in private property. In addition,

DOI: 10.4018/978-1-5225-9985-2.ch004

according to the law of 1911, it was allowed to conduct land management without "strengthening", after which the peasants also became landowners. The peasant could only sell the peasant, which limited the right to land ownership.

Organization of farms and cuts. Without land improvement, technical improvement, economic development of agriculture was impossible in the conditions of peasant stratum. In economic terms, according to Gurko's plan, strengthening without land management did not make sense.

Therefore, the work of the state land management commissions was planned to note the strips of the peasant allotment in a single section - the cut. If such a cut was far from the village, the manor was moved there and a farm was formed.

Resettlement policy has become more active in the central regions in order to solve the problem of peasant small land and reduce agrarian overpopulation. Funds were allocated for transporting people to new places, primarily to Siberia. For special settlers special passenger cars were built. Beyond the Urals, the peasants were given gratuitous land, for raising the economy and improvement, a loan was issued.

Sale of land to peasants in installments through a peasant bank was also necessary to reduce shortage of land. On the security of allotment land loans were issued for the purchase of state land transferred to the Bank's fund and land sold by the landlords.

The legislative basis of the reform was the decree of November 9, 1906, after the adoption of which the reform began.

A serious progress is being made in the peasant sector of Russia. A big role in this was played by the harvest years and the growth of world grain prices, but especially the off-farm and farm enterprises, where new technologies were used to a greater extent. The export of agricultural products increased even more in the pre-war years. Russia was the largest producer and exporter of bread and flax, a number of livestock products (Fursenko, 1965).

But this does not mean that pre-war Russia should be represented by a "peasant paradise". The problems of hunger and agrarian overpopulation were not solved. The country continued to suffer from technical, economic and cultural backwardness. The national income per capita of the agricultural population in Russia was about 52 rubles per year, and in the USA - 262 rubles.

The growth rate of labor productivity in agriculture was relatively slow. While in Russia in 1913 received 55 poods of bread from one tithe, 68 received in the United States, 89 in France, and 168 poods in Belgium. Economic growth occurred not on the basis of intensification of production, but at the expense of increasing the intensity of manual peasant labor. But in the period under review, social and economic conditions were created for the transition to a new stage of agrarian transformations-the transformation of agriculture into a capital-intensive, technologically progressive sector of the economy.

But a number of external circumstances interrupted the Stolypin reform. Stolypin himself believed that the success of his undertakings would take 15 - 20 years. But for the period 1906 - 1913 years. a lot has been done.

The community as a self-government body of the Russian village was not affected by the reform, but the socio-economic organism of the community began to collapse, the number of land communities declined from 135,000 to 110,000.

At the same time, in the central non-chernozem regions, the disintegration of the community was almost not observed, it was here that cases of arson were numerous.

There was a gradual cessation of peasant demonstrations. At the first stage of 1907 - 1909 gg. with the strengthening of allotments in the property, often under the pressure of zemstvo chiefs, the number of peasant demonstrations began to grow. But after the transfer of the emphasis of the governmental policy of land management, the refusal of coercion and some economic successes, peasant unrest has almost ceased. The main political goal was not achieved. As shown by 1917, the peasantry retained the ability "against the landlords" to "all the world". In 1917 it became obvious that the agrarian reform was late for 50 years, but the main reason for the failure was the socio-political half-hearted transformation, which was manifested in the preservation of landed estates in inviolability (Gefter, 1955).

INDUSTRIAL DEVELOPMENT OF RUSSIA AT THE BEGINNING OF THE 20TH CENTURY

To the beginning of 20th century. the territory of the Russian Empire increased to 22.2 million km. In size, it occupied the second place in the world (after the British Empire). By 1913, the population had grown to 165 million. The urban population was approximately 18% of the total number of inhabitants of Russia, which indicates that the agrarian sector of the economy still predominated in the country. At the beginning of the 20th century. the process of resettlement of the peasantry from the central to the eastern and southern regions of Russia became evident. The settlers mainly settled in the regions of Western Siberia and in the regions of the steppe belt. However, the majority of the population lived in the European part of Russia.

Russia was a multinational state, in which more than 100 different nationalities and national groups lived. The predominant place in its population was occupied by Russians (more than 40%), Ukrainians (18%), Byelorussians (4%). In the west of the country - in the Baltic States, Finland, Poland - the population had various forms of autonomy. The most complete autonomy was in Finland, where its legislation, parliament and monetary system were preserved.

In the socio-political system of Russia, old and new features intertwined. The class gradation of society and the privileged position of individual social groups were preserved. There were no democratic freedoms, the activity of political parties and trade unions was banned (until 1905). All the legislative and executive power was concentrated in the hands of the tsar, who ruled Russia and relied mainly on secession. New features in the social structure arose due to changes in the economy of the country. Modernization accelerated the formation of classes of capitalist society-the bourgeoisie and the proletariat. She also caused the erosion of class division, the change in the social status of landlords and peasants.

The nobles owned a large land fund and played a significant role in agriculture. They largely determined the political life of the country, held key posts in central and local government bodies. Under the influence of the development of capitalism, the nobility became more and more bourgeois and was ready for political cooperation with the bourgeoisie (Gindin, 1959).

Peasants were the largest social group (about 80% of the population). They were the main tax and most free estate. Before the reform of 1906 - 1910 gg. they could not freely dispose of their allotments and paid redemption payments, were subject to corporal punishment (until 1905).

Under the influence of the capitalist evolution of agriculture, the social stratification of peasants accelerated: 3% turned into a rural bourgeoisie (they were called kulaks), about 15% became hereditary. The rest of the mass led a semi-patriarchal natural economy and served as a source of hired labor in the countryside and in the cities. Despite the difference in the situation of the well-to-do and the poor, all the peasants fought against landed estates. The agrarian and peasant question remained the most acute in the political life of the country.

By 1913, the number of wage-workers amounted to approximately 18 million people, of whom 4.2 million were industrial workers.

According to V.I. Lenin, the strength of the industrial proletariat consisted in the fact that he had already formed as a class, dominated "over the center and the nerve of the entire economic system of capitalism", was the most politically conscious and organized (had his own political party).

No less remarkable was the industrial Russian bourgeoisie. It began to take shape on the basis of the commercial bourgeoisie and took shape in the class in the second half of the 19th century. It was divided into large, medium and small. The large and medium-sized was closely connected with the landowners, noblemen, needed them both economically and politically, so they sought favorable conditions for business and an alliance with tsarism. According to the census of 1897, the size of the large bourgeoisie was about 1.5 million. and 0.9 million people. - rentier (Khromov, 1950).

The petty bourgeoisie was twice as strong, more politically active. The source of its replenishment was immigrants from the artisanal, fishing industry, kulaks, stall and "petty" trade. By its political role was unstable, conjunctural. In successful profitable and profitable times, self-reliance was supported; with the deterioration of the economic state often became an ally of the proletariat. However, she always treated the big bourgeoisie with hostility. The latter was international; a significant part in it was immigrants from Germany, France, England; there were many Armenians, Azerbaijanis, Jews.

This feature objectively caused deep contradictions and acute problems in the social and economic life of society. The main ones were:

- The existence of an unlimited monarchy objectively hostile to the interests of the peoples of Russia;
- The presence of landlord landownership, which condemned the peasants of Russia to shortage of land and a low standard of living;
- The growth of national contradictions;
- A social war between the working class, the poorest peasantry against capitalist exploitation.

Social contradictions and the government's inability to solve major political problems led to a deep socio-political crisis in the early 20th century. It was expressed in the struggle of the laboring against the autocratic police system, in the creation of left-radical political parties and liberal opposition unions, in disputes within the ruling elite and fluctuations in the government's course. All these socio-political contradictions and problems have escalated in the conditions of a deep economic crisis, which Russia, like all other European powers, experienced at the beginning of the century.

The tsarist government saw the way out of the crisis in a "small victorious war". But the Russian-Japanese war (January 27, 1904 - August 23, 1905) further aggravated the political and economic situation in the country, became a powerful catalyst for the first bourgeois-democratic revolution in Russia.

The economy of Russia at the turn of the 19th - 20th centuries. Developed in the face of growing contradictions between the existing industrial-capitalist production and the semi-feudal forms of ownership and exploitation that remained in force in agriculture. The development of capitalism in Russia was hampered by an autocratic political system, the domination of landowning landownership and the class structure of society. Contrary to these factors, the economy of the country experienced an intensive growth of industrial entrepreneurship, improved organization of industrial production, its further technical re-equipment, a significant increase in the proportion of wage workers in the national economy, and an increase in their cultural and professional level (Kondakov, 1997).

In 1893, Russia began an industrial recovery, as a result of which in the early 20th century. finally formed a system of Russian capitalism with its economic, social and political characteristics.

Production growth occurred in all industries. The highest rates were in metallurgy, machine building and mining industry. Production of ferrous metallurgy for 1893 - 1899. increased more than threefold, and the increase was mainly due to new, better equipped metallurgical plants in the south of Russia. The production of machinery was also increased three-fold, the main output of which was equipment for railways.

Rapid growth rates of heavy industry demanded an increase in fuel production: oil production increased more than two and a half times, and coal - almost three times.

The rise in the field of railway construction continued, in which huge state funds were invested. For the years 1890 - 1900. The length of railways increased from 31 to 58 thousand versts. Of particular importance were the railways that linked the industrial center to the outskirts.

According to the absolute size of production, the textile industry continued to be the first to remain, but in terms of its growth rate it was considerably inferior to heavy industry.

The result of the industrial rise of 1893 - 1899 years. was not only a general increase (more than twofold) in industrial products, but also a significant concentration of production, an increase in labor productivity and the technical re-equipment of enterprises.

The industrial boom was followed by the crisis of 1900 - 1903. It embraced all the developed capitalist countries, but for Russia it turned out to be particularly difficult and time-consuming. The volume of production was reduced at all enterprises. About three thousand medium and small businesses closed. The concentration of production has increased, especially in the most important branches of industry - metallurgical, machine-building, and fuel (Moiseev, 2010).

Unlike the capitalist countries of Europe, where the ascending cycle of economic development began in 1904, replaced in 1907 by a new industrial crisis, Russia experienced a long period of economic depression. Stagnation in industrial development was due to the deterioration of the financial condition of the country as a result of the enormous costs of conducting the Russo-Japanese War of 1904-1905. and with a deficit of the state budget. Another factor that affected the economic state of the country was the revolution of 1905-1907. Mass strike movement largely disorganized production. Russian and foreign entrepreneurs, frightened by the scope of the revolution, curtailed production, the flow of funds to industry ceased.

Despite these adverse factors, for 1900 - 1908 gg. The number of workers increased by 432 thousand people, and the volume of industrial output increased by 37%.

Since the end of 1909, the period of prolonged depression has been replaced by a new industrial upswing. The highest rates of production were observed in the largest and most monopolized sectors - fuel, ferrous and nonferrous metallurgy, machine building. To a large extent, the growth in production of these industries was due to huge state orders for military needs. The improvement of the economic situation was also influenced by the high yields of 1909-1913. (with the exception of 1911); it became possible to increase the export of bread in unprecedented amounts, besides, in the world market, the price of bread increased by 35%.

During the years of industrial growth, the growth rates of production in a number of leading industries were higher than in the highly developed countries of Europe and the United States. For example, the volume of output in mechanical engineering has increased by a factor of 1.5 in these four years, and the range of machines and mechanisms has considerably expanded. The food and cotton industries developed at a high rate. The network of railways has considerably grown, which by 1913 amounted to 64 thousand versts (excluding Finland, the CER and local ones).

However, the industrial upsurge of 1909 - 1913. It did not cause the appearance of new industrial centers on the map, as it was in the late 1890s. The bulk of industrial production was concentrated in the old industrial areas, but within these areas some structural changes occurred. For example, in the Central Industrial Region, the share of heavy industry has risen substantially, the region has become a major center for machine building. Large enterprises of the textile and chemical industry have grown in the North-West region. In the Baku region, which continued to be the main oil-producing center of the country, oil engineering enterprises grew (Netesin, 1972).

In the late 19th - early 20th century in Russia, as in other capitalist countries, monopolistic associations in industry, commerce, and transport became widespread. The first monopolies arose in Russia in the 80s of the 19th century. in the metallurgical industry and in transport engineering. Organizationally, the temporary monopoly unions of the 80s and 90s were cartels, a form of association whose participants entered into an agreement on the regulation of production volumes, the conditions for the sale of products and the hiring of workers in order to extract monopoly profits. The participants of the cartel retained their industrial and commercial independence. Subsequently, most cartels grew into syndicates - associations, where the distribution of orders, the purchase of raw materials and the sale of manufactured products were carried out through a single sales office. The syndicate retained production, but the commercial independence of enterprises was lost. The highest form of monopolistic association was the trust. Trusts monopolized not only sales, but also production in a particular industry, so they combined those enterprises in which homogeneous products were produced. The enterprises that entered the trust lost their commercial and production independence.

Usually all three of these types of industrial monopolistic associations coexisted, but with the predominance of one of them. For Russia early 20th century. were characterized by associations in the form of syndicates.

The economic crisis of 1900 - 1903 years. gave a new impetus to the monopolization of industry. There are stable ties between enterprises and banks. Monopolization of industry contributed to the economic policy of the tsarist government, which saw in it a means of saving large enterprises from collapse in the years of crisis.

The largest industrial monopoly association in Russia was the syndicate "Prodamet" ("The Society for the Sale of Products of Russian Metallurgical Plants"), which arose in 1902. Although he unified no more than 20% of the factories of this industry, they produced 80% of all products for a total of 255 million rubles (data of 1910).

In 1902, the syndicate "Pipe sale" was formed, which included all the enterprises of pipe-rolling production. The monopoly association in the non-ferrous metallurgy "Copper" (1907) spoke on behalf of the trading societies, but behind it was the German-based trading company Boray, which had settled in Moscow, and received from the Russian government a monopoly on the sale of copper. Having concluded an agreement with copper-rolling plants, it deprived them of independence in buying copper and selling products from it. The monopolization reached a high level in the oil industry, where monopolistic agreements covered not only the entire domestic market, but also the export one. In this industry, there were two main companies - the Brothers Nobel partnership and the Mazut company, which were the monopolies of the highest type. In 1905, they entered into an agreement, which monopolized 77% of trade in petroleum products (Orlov, 1984).

In the coal industry, the syndicate "Produgol" ("The Society for the Trade in Mineral Fuels of the Donetsk Basin", founded in 1904) combined enterprises with 75% of all coal production in this basin.

Monopolistic associations acted in the sea and river navigation. Thus, in 1903 a syndicate called the Joint Association for the Transport and Insurance of Cargoes in Persia emerged monopolizing all cargo flows on the Caspian Sea.

The years of economic recovery (1909 - 1913) were the time of the creation of monopolies of the highest type - trusts and concerns. There were such combined associations, which included enterprises that carried out all stages of production - from the extraction of raw materials to the sale of finished products. Trestling was characteristic primarily for heavy industry, where it was carried out with the participation of government agencies.

Before the outbreak of the First World War, the monopolies had penetrated all branches of the Russian economy, in total there were about 200. The leading role among them was occupied by 30 large monopolies. Having mastered the domestic market, monopolies dictated prices and sought out exits to the foreign market. Thus, monopolistic associations have turned into the most important factor of the economic and economic life of the country.

In the early 20th century. Russia had a developed banking system. By combining industrial capital with banking, a system of financial capital was created. There were joint industrial and banking monopolies. Thus, under the control of the Russian-Asian Bank in the years of the pre-war economic recovery came the huge military-industrial concern "Putilovsky-Nevsky", an oil concern as part of AI's trusts. Mantasheva, S. G. Lianozov and the partnership "Oil", tobacco, thread and fat syndicates. In addition, several enterprises appeared in the sphere of influence of this bank.

Russia with its richest supplies of raw materials and cheap labor represented the sphere of the most profitable place for foreign capital. In the production sphere, foreign capital was directed primarily to heavy industry. Its size in such industries as mining, metalworking and machine building exceeded Russian capital investments. Significant was the share of foreign investment in construction and the chemical industry. Despite Russia's financial dependence on foreign capital, the Russian economy maintained its independence and independently determined the direction of development.

Despite the intensive development of industry, Russia remained predominantly an agrarian country. In the years 1900 - 1913. agricultural production grew by 34%. Although the share of income from agriculture has declined slightly over the years, it continued to dominate the country's economy.

In the early 20th century. landlordism continued to decline. In 1906 - 1916 years. of 51 million dessiatines of the noble land, 9.5 million were sold to the Peasant Bank and 8.8 million were pledged at the Noble Bank. The landlord economy was characterized by a tendency to increase its marketability. The share of landlord grain on the grain market has steadily increased. This was facilitated by an increase in its agrotechnical level and favorable conditions in the international bread market. 81% of the landed estates employed wage-labor, and at the same time the mass of small landowners conducted their farming in the old manner - by letting a part of the land lease for work with the use of primitive peasant implements (Petrov, 2001).

The main productive force in agriculture in Russia in the early 20th century. The peasantry remained, which was 3/4 of the country's population. The share of peasant farming accounted for 88% of the gross grain harvest and about 50% of marketable grain. The provision of allotment land of the peasantry was extremely uneven. According to the land census of 1905, 137 million dessiatines of land were in communal and household ownership of peasants. About half of it (64 million dessiatins) was in the hands of the well-to-do peasantry, which amounted to 1/6 of the households. Such unevenness in land maintenance caused significant property differences in the village.

The development of the productive forces in the peasant economy proceeded slowly. The main obstacle in the case of low agrotechnics was peasant small land. It worsened due to the natural growth of the rural population and the fragmentation of peasant households by the growth of family sections.

The struggle between peasants and landlords continued to remain at the beginning of the 20th century. the main content of social contradictions in the countryside. The peasant movement increasingly took on an agrarian orientation. If in 1870 - 1880 years. 43% of peasant unrest appeared on agrarian soil (170 out of 400), in 1881 - 1890 years. 67% (425 out of 630), then in 1891 - 1900 years. - more than 77% (400 of 515). Land disputes with landlords, the destruction of landmarks on the boundaries of possessions, the plowing of landlords' lands, resistance to surveyors in surveying land, collision with the administration of landed estates become commonplace and they eventually led to a revolution (Rapatskaya, 2002).

THE CAUSES AND CONSEQUENCES OF REVOLUTIONS IN RUSSIA

The revolution lasted 2.5 years (from January 9, 1905 to June 3, 1907). Unlike European revolutions, the Russian one had its own peculiarities, which in many respects were due to the fact that in the society there was a polarization of the classes.

1. It took place not at dawn, but already in the period of developed, mature capitalism (imperialism). Hence its tactics - to press the autocracy, but not to overthrow it, to make tsarism give the bourgeoisie better conditions for big business. This tactic was distinguished by political criticism of the autocratic-feudal system and at the same time by the desire for economic cooperation, the desire to use the state guarding apparatus if the workers "become insolent" and begin an active struggle against bourgeois exploitation.

For these reasons, the bourgeoisie was not and could not be revolutionary, could not be the leader and the driving force of the revolution.

2. By the forms of struggle and by the role of the working class in it, the revolution was proletarian. The working class was politically active (it had its own party armed with revolutionary theory), organized by the most advanced technology of machine production. Working forms of struggle-strikes, strikes-were widely used by other sections of the population of the city and the countryside. The workers had nothing to lose, except the chains. Low level of well-being, long (10-14 hours) working day, poor working conditions (night shifts, use of female and child labor, high accidents, fines, absence of proper labor laws, pensions, disability from unfortunates cases) made them resolute and ready to bring the revolution to the resolution of all the contradictions of society.

January 3, 1905 began a long-prepared strike at the Putilov plant in St. Petersburg. The workers demanded an increase in wages, the cancellation of compulsory overtime and the establishment of an 8-hour working day. They were supported by other factories and plants in St. Petersburg, and on January 8, the strike already covered 111,000 workers in the capital, taking a general character. At this time, in the organization of George Gapon, a plan was developed to arrange a peaceful procession to the Tsar to file a petition on the needs of the workers. "We, the workers of St. Petersburg," the petition said, "our wives and children and helpless old parents came to you, sir, to seek truth and protection. We have become poor, we are oppressed, we are burdened with excessive work, they abuse us, they do not recognize us as people, they treat us like slaves who must endure bitter fate and remain silent. We were silent, but the limit of patience came ... ". At the insistence of the Social Democrats (Mensheviks), apart from economic demands, political ones were included in the petition: political amnesty, personal immunity, freedom of speech, press, assembly, equality before the law, permission to create professional labor unions.

The First Congress of Soviets was held on June 3 (16), 1917, in Petrograd. Most of them belonged to the Mensheviks and Socialist-Revolutionaries. The Congress adopted the Socialist-Revolutionary Menshevik resolutions, in particular, on trusting the Provisional Government (Rudyuk, 1999).

On the morning of October 25, 1917, the Military Revolutionary Committee declared the Provisional Government deposed on behalf of the Petrograd Soviet. The Second All-Russian Congress of Soviets, which opened in the evening of the same day, at which delegates from 402 Soviets of Russia were represented, sanctioned the transfer of power to the Soviets. Of the 670 delegates to the congress, 390 were Bolsheviks, 160 Socialist-Revolutionaries, 72. Mensheviks, and 38 belonged to other parties. The overwhelming majority of delegates supported the Congress decision.

The first decrees of the Soviet government were approved at the congress: the "Decree on Peace", which suggested that all countries participating in the war, their peoples, governments, begin negotiations on peace;

"Decree on the land," drawn up on the basis of 242 peasant orders, according to which landlord ownership of land was abolished; the principle of equal land use was introduced. The congress formed a new composition of the Central Executive Committee of the Soviets (LB Kamenev became chairman):

62 Bolsheviks, 29 left Socialist-Revolutionaries, six social-democrats-internationalists, three Ukrainian socialists and one maximalist. The Congress was formed and the first Soviet government - the Council of People's Commissars (the head of the government was VI Lenin). The events of October 25-26 (November 7-8) 1917 opened new pages in the political history of the peoples of multinational Russia.

Until now, interest has not diminished by 1917, especially by the October days, and it has increased considerably in the conditions of perestroika and the post-perestroika period of the political development of the Russian state.

October 1917 was reflected in many thousands of books, pamphlets, articles, in documentary publications and memoirs. However, his political history is still not objectively and in detail written. Meanwhile, the overwhelming majority of the mass media are increasingly giving examples of the application of the well-known formula (Ryabenko, 2014).

"History is politics, overturned in the past." At the same time, a significant place is given to many problems related to October 1917. The conjuncture of the current policy is increasingly replacing the pluralism of opinions and assessments.

Many questions now cause controversy and debate, including the following: Was the October Revolution legitimate and did the Bolsheviks commit violence against history? Was it possible then not a revolutionary, but a reformist way out of the political crisis of Russian society? The answers to these questions, like to other questions, are far from being the same, and at times diametrically opposed.

We will begin by stressing that the February events of 1917 were the beginning of a powerful process, the completion of which could not but go beyond the framework of this revolutionary year. The fall of the autocracy has exposed the depth of political, social and economic contradictions and simultaneously generated a rise in expectations and claims of a social nature for the overwhelming majority of the population that makes up the most deprived part of society. High political, social and civic activity, awareness of their interests by the individual and the need for joint actions for their implementation are a characteristic feature of this period. On the one hand, there was a huge discrepancy between the "desire of the masses of the multinational country to meet their demands due to poverty, the national oppression of the autocracy, military ruin, on the other - weaknesses, fluctuations in power even in those issues that were completely legal. this inevitably led to a wide application of revolutionary action: an eight-hour working day was introduced by a by-pass, the workers sought the right to participate in the management of enterprises, peasants taking over and landed estates. And as the war went on, the weapon was more than enough (Rykalov, 1978).

In the autumn of 1917, peasant insurrections with the demand for land covered the whole of the European part of the country, the army refused to fight, workers' strikes undermined the scarcely alive industry. Although the crisis of the government was overcome by the beginning of September, it was no longer able to seize the political situation, as it did not enjoy the confidence and support of the majority of the population. The masses saw in the Soviets the opportunity to realize their demands for democracy and social justice. Their significance has increased dramatically, in many places they have become the actual power. In the Soviets themselves, those who advocated the transfer of power to them in the center and on the ground became the most influential. They were Bolsheviks and Left SRs.

CONCLUSION

After the October Revolution, the possibility of combining the Soviets with the parliamentary system sharply decreased. Supporters of the Western choice, with the support of the most conservative forces, began an armed struggle with the Soviets. Nevertheless, some moments - the attempts to form a homogeneous socialist government, the bipartisan Soviet government (almost immediately after the victory of October), the convocation of the Constituent Assembly (unsuccessful not through the fault of the new authorities) - inspired the hope that the Soviets would still be able to inculcate elements of parliamentarism. Such an outcome to a certain extent would preserve the democratic choice made by the people in the course of the revolution, would allow to ensure the unity of society and prevent the uncontrolled disintegration of the state, gradually transforming the process into civilized forms. However, this turned out to be unrealizable, in which to some extent all parties, all the forces of the opposite camps, including the same Western "civilized" countries (intervention, occupation, robbery of temporarily occupied territories) are guilty to a certain extent.

REFERENCES

Gindin, I. F. (1959). On the economic policy of the tsarist government in the 60's and 80's 19th century. *Voprosy Istorii, 5,* 63-82.

Glushenko, I. I. (1963). *The economic expansion of foreign capital in the Far East and the end of the 19th and beginning of the 20th. In On the peculiarities of imperialism in Russia*, 410-418. Publishing House of the Academy of Sciences of the USSR.

Ilina, T.V. (1994). *Art History. Russian art.* Academic Press. (in Russian)

Ioann (Snychev). (2001). Met. Russian symphony. Academic Press. (in Russian)

Kabytov, P. S., Kozlov, V. A., & Litvak, B. G. (1988). Russian peasantry: the stages of spiritual liberation. Academic Press.

Kanishcheva, N. I. (1982). On the question of the socio-economic background of the Great October Revolution in the coverage of modern bourgeois historiography of Germany. *Voprosy of German history,* 104-109.

Khromov, P. A. (1950). The economic development of Russia in the 19th-20th centuries. Academic Press.

Kiselev, G. S. (1992). *The tragedy of society and man. An attempt to understand the experience of Soviet history*. Academic Press. (in Russian)

Kondakov, I. V. (1997). *Introduction to the history of Russian culture*. Academic Press. (in Russian)

Kovalchenko, I. D. (1971). The ratio of peasant and landlord farming in the agricultural production of capitalist Russia. *Problems of socio-economic history,* 171-194.

Kravchenko, A. I. (2005). Culturology. Academic Press. (in Russian)

Laverychev, V. Y. (1967). On the other side of the barricades (from the history of the struggle of the Moscow bourgeoisie against the revolution). Academic Press.

Moiseev, V. V. (2010). Russian history (2nd ed.). Moscow, Russia: Moscow Institute of Economics, Management and Law. (in Russian)

Netesin, Y. N. (1972). On the peculiarities of the reproduction of Russian industrial capital at the beginning of the 20th century The problem of multistructure. *Voprosy of the history of capitalist Russia*, 47-56.

Orlov, M. N. (1984). Development of mining and mining industry in Eastern Siberia and the Far East in the era of imperialism (1898-1917). *Manuscript Diss. Cand. ist spider.*

Petrov, Y. A. (2001). *The problem of public debt and private German investments in Russia Economic history of Russia 19th-20th centuries: a modern look*. Academic Press.

Pogrebinsky, A. P. (1963). *The controversial issues of studying state-monopoly capitalism in pre-revolutionary Russia On the features of imperialism in Russia* (pp. 124–148). Publishing House of the Academy of Sciences of the USSR.

Rapatskaya, L. A. (2002). Russian Art Culture: Study Guide. Academic Press. (in Russian)

Rudyuk, N. V. (1999). Banking unions in Russia at the turn of the 19th-20th centuries Russia at the turn of the 19th-20th centuries. *Materials of scientific readings in memory of Professor V.I. Bovykin*, 148-166.

Ryabenko, V. (2014). *Soviet culture in the years of the Great Patriotic War and in the post-war period.* Retrieved from https://magref.ru/sovetskaya-kultura-v-godyi-velikoy-otechestvennoy-voynyi-i-v-poslevoennyiy-period (in Russian)

Chapter 5
The Development of Russia in the Early Years of Soviet Power

Bogdan Ershov
Voronezh State Technical University, Russia

ABSTRACT

This chapter discusses the reasons for the victory of the Russian revolution of 1917, as well as the first steps of the Soviet government to reform the country. It is shown that the revolution had a bourgeois-democratic nature. Different opinions of scientists on recognition and non-recognition of the Russian revolution of 1917 are revealed. Historical analysis has shown that Russia reached "a certain height" of capitalism in large-scale industry, in transport, and in the economy, where, as in the West, capitalist monopolies and large banks dominated. As for the village, it was still on the eve of the bourgeois-democratic revolution, and there could be no question of any preconditions for socialism.

INTRODUCTION

It should not be forgotten that after the October Revolution, Finland, Poland, Lithuania, Latvia, Estonia, Bessarabia declared independence, which joined Romania in February 1918. "Civilized" is all this - another question. But without the consent of the Soviets, the Soviet government is unlikely that these countries would be able to obtain their independence, although it was declared by them.

DOI: 10.4018/978-1-5225-9985-2.ch005

In the conditions of a complex class, military, diplomatic, social and economic situation in Soviet Russia, a strictly centralized system of power began to be formed (practically forcedly). It had a pronounced non-Western, noncapitalist character. It was directed against the propertied classes, private property, the market. At the same time, the formation of a rigid organization of power took place on the foundation of the Bolshevik party. Why this particular party? The point is not only that it formed a government (although this is an important fact), but rather that in those conditions only the Bolshevik Party retained the All-Russian organization - cells in factories, factories, in the countryside, factions in the Soviets, trade unions and other mass organizations. The Bolsheviks had efficient structures at all levels. The party was strictly centralized and educated in the spirit of rigorous discipline, had at its disposal armed people (revolutionary soldiers, sailors, detachments of the Red Guard) (Semennikova, 1994).

In the publications of contemporary subjective political scientists and publicists, words with an insulting tone towards the revolutionary masses of the people are very often encountered: revolt, lumpen, crowd, ochlocracy. These accusations do not correspond to historical reality. Obviously, they try to give out wishful thinking. Historical facts show the opposite, namely: the October Revolution is the democratic choice of the majority of the Russian people. Let us cite a number of other points of view of domestic and foreign historians on the evaluation and significance of the October Revolution.

HISTORIOGRAPHY AND ANALYSIS OF THE RUSSIAN REVOLUTION OF 1917

Appeal to the works of foreign historians about the economic and social consequences of the industrial and agrarian development of Russia in the second half of the 19th and early 20th centuries, undoubtedly, will allow a better understanding of the strengths and weaknesses of foreign Russian studies in general in order to reveal its achievements and problems. It is also necessary for a more complete and comprehensive study of the historical experience of the capitalist development of Russia — a topic whose meaning and significance is beyond doubt. But a complete study of the entire foreign historiography of this issue is an extremely complex and diverse task. In view of this, the intercultural way of studying historical literature on this issue seems preferable.

A prominent place in the first stage of domestic research is occupied by the fundamental monograph by Rashina "The Population of Russia for 100 Years (1811–1913): Statistical Essays," which contains a special section "The dynamics of the number and processes of formation of the urban population of Russia in the 19th and early 20th centuries.", Which analyzes data mainly on capitals and cities . Valuable statistical data on the dynamics of the number and mechanisms of formation of the urban population, its growth factors, age and sex composition and literacy in the 19th-early 20th centuries. centuries, contain historical and demographic works B.V. Tikhonova. In them, on the basis of Lenin's methods, the number of the main social and professional groups of the population in a number of cities of the Russian Empire is determined, the connection of demographic processes and the socio-economic development of the country is shown (Shatsillo, 1961).

Factors that had an important and sometimes decisive influence on the fate of the city center, not without reason, should include its location in the country, the availability of convenient means of communication, the climatic features of a particular region, geography, the proximity of minerals, etc. In this connection, works on historical geography are of great importance for the study of the socio-economic development of Russian cities in the second half of the 19th and early 20th centuries. In their work, V. Z. Drobizhev, I. D. Kovalchenko, and A. V. Muravyov were among the first in the Soviet historiography who gave a generalizing characteristic of the historical and geographical conditions of the country's development.

Of great importance for the study of the socio-economic development of the urban centers of the Black Soil Region in the second half of the 19th and early 20th centuries are works devoted to the study of the development of transport systems in the country. Navigation along the Volga and its tributaries is considered in the book of Shubin. The development of rail transport in the 19th century. in Russia the work of A.I. Solovieva. The author considers the creation of the railway network as an integral part of the industrial revolution in Russia. A significant place in the study of A.I. Solovyov was devoted to the construction and operation of the Volga-Don Railway, Tambov-Saratov, Morshansk-Syzran, Moscow-Kazan and others, which were of great importance for the Tambov province and the country as a whole and contributed to the transformation of a number of urban centers of this region into the largest industrial transport knots.

Ethnosocial processes in cities, including those that occurred in the post-reform period, attract the growing attention of researchers, which was noted, on the one hand, by the violation of many norms of traditional life, and on the other, by the emergence of new everyday traditions. These issues, in particular, are devoted to the work of Anokhin and Shmelev, Budin, Kupriyanov, Yukhnev.

Today there is a considerable amount of research devoted to the analysis of foreign historiography of the capitalist development of the Russian Empire. However, the works of English-speaking authors were and remain in the center of attention of Russian historians of both the Soviet and post-Soviet period. This approach is largely justified - it was the Anglo-American researchers who developed and formulated theoretical constructions that formed the basis for a specific study of the economic and social history of Russia. As for the last decade, there is every reason to talk about the influence of these theories, especially "modernization", on studies published in Russia — it is enough to name the works of Igritsky, Mironov, Alekseyev, Krasilitsikov, Senevsky and others. But with all the justification of interest in the English-speaking historiography of the history of Russia, one should not lose sight of the development of Russian studies in other states, especially in Germany (Sidorov, 1998).

Due to a number of circumstances, this country is characterized by a significant interest in Russia and its history. At the beginning of the 20th century, it was in Germany that the largest number of works in foreign Europe came out, one way or another affecting the problems of the economic and partly social development of then-Russia. Many of these works are not only historiographic, but also of primary importance - their authors visited Russia and operated on data obtained from the press, narrative and statistical sources.

Academician of the Russian Academy of Sciences P. G. Volobuev writes that it would be wrong to deny the fact that in the course of its development in Russia, capitalism has significantly advanced the country forward in an economic, mainly industrial, respect. By the beginning of the world war, Russia occupied the fifth place in the world in terms of the general level of industrial production. He notes that Russian capitalism could not solve the task of industrializing the country, but only laid its foundations. At the same time, industrial progress was bought at the cost of ruin of the village, mass raskrestyanivaniya. The great power did not possess a developed machine-building. Capitalism did not have time to rebuild the bourgeois economy - the main branch of the national economy of Russia, it was dominated by the forms of primitive capitalism, not to mention the domination of the remnants of serfdom.

In our journalism, as the academician writes, he insists that in the pre-war years (1909-1913) Russia annually exported 9-14 million tons of grain, that is, in contrast to the present time, a major grain exporter. And at the same time, a huge part of the rural, peasant population of the empire systematically undernourished, lived in poverty, poverty, doomed to illiteracy and darkness. And in 1911 another crop failure broke out that swept across 20 provinces of the European part of Russia. Hunger and needed food aid, according to official figures, 20 million people. And modern political scientists should have known that the export of grain was carried out through under-consumption, malnutrition of the masses, and not because of an overabundance of agricultural products. It was necessary to translate the development of capitalism from the "Russian-Prussian" path to the advanced "American."

It is also characteristic that the Russian bourgeoisie was afraid of a bourgeois-democratic revolution. True, Stolypin, who was exorbitantly praised today, wanted to clean up the soil for the development of capitalism from above, but according to the old, most conservative "Prussian" way, and thereby speed up this development. Due to ignorance, our publicists, including economists, portray him as a supporter of the farmer variant of agrarian-capitalist evolution (Smetanii, 2002).

During the First World War, the system of Russian capitalism could not withstand military tension and entered a period of acute crisis. In 1917, this crisis took the form of disintegration, not foreseen by any theory, the disintegration of not only the capitalist relations and the productive forces (industry, transport, finance), but also the functioning of the entire national economic organism. Russia was facing a national catastrophe.

From the point of view of "classical" Marxism, a high level of productive forces is necessary for the accomplishment of the socialist revolution and the transition to socialism, which became tightly within the framework of capitalist production relations. In this sense, the October Revolution did not take place "according to Marx." But it happened "according to Lenin," which, based on the realities of the new historical era, substantially corrected Marxism on this issue. In particular, he rejected the postulate of a direct, direct dependence between the readiness of a single capitalist country to socialism and the high level of development of the productive forces.

It is known that Lenin did not base his plans on these hopes alone. His concrete historical analysis showed that Russia has reached a "certain height" of capitalism, and in large-scale industry, transport, and economy, where, like in the West, capitalist monopolies and large banks dominated. As for the village, it was still on the eve of the bourgeois-democratic revolution and there could be no question of any prerequisites for socialism. Therefore, Lenin's socialist project did not provide for the immediate "introduction" of socialism in Russia, since the country for this in general was not economically prepared, but proceeded from the need to begin transitional steps and measures leading to socialism (nationalization of banks, monopolies and lands, workers' control over production etc.).

So, Russia was the first to complete the socialist revolution not because of its relatively low capitalist development. As Lenin correctly noted, "our backwardness has moved us forward."

The February revolution, having overthrown tsarism, could not at the same time solve the basic general democratic and national tasks (on peace, on land, on combating economic dislocation and hunger, and other issues). This became an internal spring for the development of the revolutionary process in the socialist direction. The October Revolution in those conditions represented our Russian, different from the West European option, the path to modern industrial civilization.

Here is the point of view of Y. A. Polyakova. He believes that the question of the possibility of a coalition between the Bolsheviks and other socialist parties acquired particular importance. In his opinion, in principle, it was desirable and possible. But the Coalition coalition is different. Its content depends on the situation, on the correlation of forces. The question of the coalition arose even before October, and at the end of 1917 it practically did not go off the agenda, almost every week acquiring new forms and filling with new content. At the Second Congress of Soviets, the right-wing Mensheviks and Socialist-Revolutionaries proposed to begin negotiations with the Provisional Government on the formation of a Cabinet that would rely on all sectors of society. But the Provisional Government was already overthrown, and attempts to revive it led to a complete denial of the victory of the revolution. Such a coalition would be simply ridiculous. Therefore, the congress did not accept the proposals of the Right Socialist-Revolutionaries, and they left the congress (Stepanov, 1993).

Moreover, even after the formation of the Soviet one-party government, the question of the socialist coalition rose with renewed vigor and acquired new forms. The very fact that the discussion of the coalition issue led to the first serious crisis in the leadership of the Bolshevik party, speaks of the extreme importance of this issue. Polyakov believes that this time not all opportunities for compromise were used. The Bolsheviks could make concessions. But the socialist forces were too heterogeneous. Nevertheless, a coalition with all truly revolutionary forces, despite the difficulties, was still possible. Although the bloc with the Left SRs eventually ended in failure, it at some point played a positive role, and most importantly - showed the possibility of uniting the left forces.

Finally, let us quote the point of view of a foreign scientist. A.E. Rabinovich, a professor at the Indian University (USA), stresses: "I consider the October Revolution to be one of the most important events of the 20th century. It not only became a turning point in the history of Russia itself, but also had a huge influence in our century, both positive and negative, on the fate of Europe. In particular, the fear of communism, in my opinion, made it possible for certain circles in Germany to bring Hitler to power. As for the second part of the question - whether October was a tragedy, then, with certainty I can say that no.

I see two main reasons for the victory of the Bolsheviks. The first is that the Bolshevik party in 1917 was a democratic and centralized organization that had broad ties with the masses. The Bolsheviks, better than other parties, knew the masses, their aspirations. The second reason, directly stemming from the first, is that the program of actions of the Bolsheviks proceeded from the knowledge of the masses. The slogans put forward by the Bolshevik Party reflected most of all the desire of the people: peace, land to the peasants, power to the Soviets!

In such a complex and tense situation it was necessary to solve the first urgent tasks, including the consolidation of Soviet power, the formation of the political system of society, the implementation of new socio-economic transformations. The difficulty of solving them was due to a number of reasons, the main one being that the construction of a new society had to be carried out in unknown ways and alone. The situation was further complicated by the fact that many leaders of the October Revolution proposed to be guided by the doctrine of the world proletarian revolution. Among them was the leader of the Bolsheviks, Lenin.

The fact is that international events after October developed in such a way that a revolutionary situation developed in Europe, and it seemed that a big spark was needed to spark a world revolutionary fire. For the Russian Bolsheviks, this was very important, since they viewed the revolutionary events in Russia as the first victorious act of the world socialist revolution. And in the world revolution and the help of the proletariat of the advanced countries, Lenin and other Bolshevik leaders saw a means of solving the difficult tasks of building socialism in Russia (Tarnovsky, 1990).

THE FIRST ACTIVITIES OF THE SOVIET GOVERNMENT

But what they wanted did not happen, although the Russian example aroused a powerful revolutionary wave that swept in 1918-1921. in many countries. Nevertheless, in the hope of an early victory of the world revolution, the Bolsheviks launched work to solve the priority tasks of building a new society, organizing its defense. This work began in a difficult period, when the Mensheviks and Socialist-Revolutionaries tried to liquidate the Soviet power by "peaceful means". Their support was Vikzhel - the All-Russian Executive Committee of the Railway Workers' Union. The leadership of Vikzhel in the first days of Soviet power stated in an ultimatum form that in order to avoid a civil war it recognized as legitimate the creation of a homogeneous socialist government in which all socialist parties must take part - from the Bolsheviks to the people's socialists (SRs). For the Bolshevik leadership it was obvious that a political agreement with the socialist parties was practically impossible, but nevertheless the Central Committee went to negotiations with Vikzhel. At the talks, the delegation of the Central Committee of the Bolsheviks, contrary to the party decision, supported Vikzhel's idea of creating a government in which the Bolsheviks were given a secondary role. This behavior of the Bolshevik delegation caused the condemnation of the majority of party members. In response, some members of the Central Committee withdrew from its composition. Several members of the Soviet government also resigned.

So there was the first crisis of the Soviet government. But the Extraordinary All-Russian Congress of Railway Workers, held in December 1917, in turn, condemned the policy of the Vikzhel leadership and called for the support of the Soviet government. In December, an agreement was reached on the entry of seven representatives of the Left Socialist Revolutionaries (SRs) into the Soviet government (Sovnarkom), which was 1/3 of its composition. This governmental bloc was necessary to consolidate Soviet power, to attract broad masses of peasants to its side, among which the Left SRs enjoyed strong support at the initial stage.

The immediate task of the Soviet government was the creation of the organs of protection of the Soviet Republic. To this end, the protection of public order was entrusted to the workers 'and peasants' militia. For the continuous struggle against subversive activities, sabotage and speculation, a resolution of the Council of People's Commissars of December 7 established the All-Russian Extraordinary Commission (VChK), headed by F.E. Dzerzhinsky.

The decree of the Council of People's Commissars of November 22, 1917 provided for the creation of people's courts and revolutionary tribunals, and by decrees on January 15 and 29, 1918, the beginning of the creation of the Workers 'and Peasants' Red Army and Red Navy.

About the fate of the Constituent Assembly, we can say the following: in the elections held in mid-November 1917, about 50 political parties of Russia participated, with the Bolsheviks receiving 22.5% of votes, moderate socialist parties - 60.5 (of whom more than 55% are socialists -revolutionaries), the bourgeois parties - 17. The results of the elections were explained by the fact that they were conducted on the lists compiled by these parties even before the October events. Right-wing and left-wing Social Revolutionaries then acted as a single party with a common list of candidates. Now the Left SRs have joined the coalition. Thus it turned out that the bulk of voters voted for a party that no longer existed. This meant that the distribution of seats did not reflect changes in the alignment of political forces in the country, which occurred on the eve and during the October events (Volobuev, 1956).

The Soviet government recognized the independence of Finland, Ukraine, Poland, the peoples of the Baltic states. In those days it was unprecedented in the history of the existing empires political act. And this is the preferred one of today, to be remembered, or even perverse, in the form of the so-called national liberation. Meanwhile, at the present time Finland and Poland separated from Russia and formed independent states with the consent of the Soviet government, and in December 1922 the rest voluntarily joined the Union of Soviet Socialist Republics. However, political and socioeconomic transformations in Russia, immediately after the victory of the revolution, suffered in the difficult conditions of the aggravation of the class struggle within the country and the confrontation that was flared by the leading world powers. Thus, a peculiarity of the Russian revolution of 1917 was its peculiar overgrowth from the stage of the bourgeois-democratic (or popular-labor, as the Socialist-Revolutionary Party defined it) to the socialist revolution, as it was previously called. What is the characteristic of this transition, how did this happen and what forces led this coup. Having failed to oppose the Bolsheviks with any real power in the autumn of 1917, most of the representatives of the moderate liberalism and the liberalization of the revolution, began to hold the position that the Bolsheviks "distort the revolution" and that "the conquests of the revolution "are carried out in Russia, in spite of, and not because of them. The way out of this difficult and at the first time was in the theory of the "two revolutions" - the beneficent of October, "somebody and somehow imposed." The position of this combination of "recognition" and "non-recognition" of the Russian Revolution of 1917 continued to be partially preserved in emigration. Most of the representatives of the socialist parties who did not accept the Bolshevik version of the revolution and who were trying to protect socialism from "Bolshevik perversions" and representatives of the liberal trend who "judged" the revolution and, ultimately, the positive thought of the Russian revolution, 1917, for the fate of Russia, and somewhere else Europe (Voslensky, 1991).

The problem of the contradictory character of the Russian revolution of 1917 was also the subject of a discussion among representatives of Russian social and political thought. According to S.L. Frank, this was "the main tragic misunderstanding of the Russian revolution, the peculiar content of its tragic meaninglessness." For this revolution was based on the democratic movement, which began with the liberation of the peasants in the spontaneous process of everyday "democratization", the penetration of the lower strata into all spheres of social, state, cultural life, the process, by the "the desire of the peasantry for independence and autonomy, t .e. in essence, proprietary instincts." Socialism, noted SL. Frank, carried away the masses "not with his positive ideal, but with his force of repulsion from the old system". Ultimately, revolutionary socialism as the degeneration of the West European proletarian movement, ideologically impregnated with "rebellious and religious eschatology - with its teaching about the class struggle and its leap into the" realm of freedom "- has become an adequate expression of the long- standing primordial Russian peasant-raznochinsky sense of enmity nobility and its culture. "The masses were not to socialism, but simply to the division of bourgeois wealth, and socialism was successful because of its political tendencies. "In essence, concluded SL., Frank, it was an all-Russian pugachevshchina early 20 century." "According to the philosopher, on the part of the perception of socialism," the Russian revolution, according to its internal socio-political essence, is a painful crisis of the sharp democratization of Russia, no more, but no less. "

Thus, it is possible to single out specific features of the Russian revolutionary process that determined its catastrophic nature:

- The original anarchism of the masses, held by the regime of violence in a state of passive submission;
- The decline of the ruling class, condemned by history to death, but hoping for salvation by eliminating the shaken autocracy;
- The theoretical maximalism of the revolutionary intelligentsia, prone to utopian decisions and devoid of political experience;

- Separatist aspirations of national elites;
- Psychological features of the national genotype, prone to a delayed reaction to external stimuli, and therefore condensing in itself a charge of psychological energy, breaking through in the form of revolutionary explosions (Voslensky, 1991).

Thus, the democratic alternative, which for eight months of 1917 had managed to transform itself from a liberal-democratic to a radically democratic one, did not materialize. Too heavy a legacy for the new Russia was the world war, as well as the long-standing acute crisis of the system, not overcome by the fall of the autocracy, and in some ways even reinforced by this act. In 1917, the revolutionary process was growing, as a result of the turbulent, largely spontaneous flow. The sharp increase in radicalism, and sometimes even the bitter enmity of the masses, combined with the remnants of the traditional communal-egalitarian mass consciousness, has made the unrealistic liberal-democratic alternative associated with the formation of a stable political regime and civil society. Liberal democracy failed to combine legislative work on the introduction of parliamentarism with the implementation of effective external and especially domestic policies. In the fall of 1917, the masses could no longer convince logically irreproachable arguments of legal experts on the constructiveness of parliamentary democracy (Zamaraev, 2016).

CONCLUSION

Summing up the work done, it can be stated that the formation of the principles of the Bolshevik social policy passed a long period from the birth of the party to its coming to power. The legal formulation of the norms elaborated in the Constitution of the RSFSR of 1918 is being completed. The party initially relied on global social transformations that were to lead to the formation of a classless society. And here they were direct followers of the founders of Marxism. However, the main place in their ideology was immediately taken by the demand for the conquest of political power, without waiting until the necessary economic preconditions for establishing the dictatorship of the proletariat were formed. The main content of the activities of the RSDRP (b) before coming to power was the struggle to attract as many supporters of their party as possible. Gradually, in resolutions, appeals and other documents, there was a transition of ideological justification from the general democratic requirements for strict forms and methods of social policy. The coming to power created a new practical reality, which expressed an urgent need to keep power in their hands. The narrowness of the social base led the Bolsheviks at the beginning of 1918 to substantiate the predominant role of revolutionary violence in asserting the foundations of the dictatorship of the proletariat. The choice of forms, methods and tools of social policy in relation to the urban population was closely connected with the social structure of cities, the demographic processes taking place in them and the assessment of the behavior of citizens. Along with the existence of estates, classes — the bourgeoisie and the proletariat — were formed in the cities. Forced urbanization processes at the beginning of 20 c. have not led yet to the established social psychology of new classes. First of all it concerned the workers.

The First World War and the subsequent socioeconomic crisis directly affected the demographic processes in cities. First of all, the natural increase in the first one and a half years of the war is replaced by a reduction in the number and gender-age disproportion of the population. The mobilization of men leads to the dominance of the female population and age groups up to 20 years. The increased influx of refugees evacuated from the western provinces of Russia to the cities and the influx of migrants from the countryside led to an increase in the number of marginalized among the urban population who were ready to support any authority that promises to improve their situation. Analysis of the content of the Bolshevik policy during the civil war showed that taking into account the real socio-demographic and behavioral situation had a decisive influence on the choice of specific forms, methods and tools for its implementation (Ershov, 2018).

The economic development of Russia during this period entailed a period of large-scale changes, the reasons for which were largely due to its distinct originality at the turn of the two centuries. In Russia, capitalism is being established at an accelerated pace. However, the process of the capitalist development of Russia in many significant indicators differs markedly from the classical, Western European variant.

Domestic industry grew at a high rate. Accelerated economic growth was largely promoted by the policy of forced industrialization of the country, which was primarily associated with the name of Witte S.Yu., one of the largest statesmen of the last decades of the Russian Empire, who occupied in 1892-1903. post of finance minister.

In general, the overall results of the development of domestic industry in the late 19-early 20 centuries. Were quite impressive. In terms of industrial production, Russia in 1913 took the 5th place in the world. In the agrarian sector of the economy, personality played an important role - Stolypin P.A. During the years of reform, the marketability of peasant farms has significantly increased due to farms and cuts. Introduced new farming systems and crops. From one third to one half of the individual farmers participated in credit unions, which gave them the means to modernize. In general, there was no revolution in agroeconomics, but when assessing economic results, it is important to clarify the direction and gain momentum. In socio-political terms, the reform was a relative success. The community as an organ of self-government of the Russian village was not affected by the reform, but the social and economic body of the community began to collapse. The multistructure of the economy caused an abundance of social strata and groups, a large number of people with temporary social status. The peasantry remained the most numerous class in the social structure of the country, and its number continued to increase at the beginning of the 20th century, despite the increased outflow of population to the city, although at a slower pace than before (Zezina, 1990).

The rapid growth of the Russian industry in the late 19-early 20 centuries. accompanied by an increase in the number of industrial proletariat. The composition of the working class of Russia was heterogeneous. In large-scale industry, hereditary proletarians prevailed. In construction, water transport, and so on, there were many recent immigrants from the village. In general, the relationship of workers with agriculture has steadily weakened, and the share of those for whom work in industry was the main occupation increased. By the beginning of the 20th century, a rapid increase in the population of the Russian Empire could be noted. During this period, it increased from 125.6 million to 159.2 million people (by 33.4%). The average life expectancy has increased from 27 to 33 years.

Thus, our analysis of the socio-economic policy of Russia showed that almost all of its areas were of a pronounced liberal-bourgeois character. Thanks to a rational and purposeful policy pursued by the Ministry of Finance (transformation and development of the tax system, customs protection, attracting foreign capital, streamlining public debt and money circulation), the industrial revolution in Russia was completed, which contributed to the development of industrial production.

REFERENCES

Ashmarov, I. A., & Ershov, B. A. (2018). Church as a social and economic institution of society in the 19th-early 20th centuries. *II International Scientific and Practical Conference "Orthodoxy and Society: the Edge of Interaction." Chita: Transbaikal State University,* 33-41. (in Russian)

Ashmarov, I. A., Ershov, B. A., Bulavin, R. V., Shkarubo, S. N., & Danilchenko, S. (2018). The Material And Financial Situation Of The Russian Orthodox Church In The 19th-early 20th centuries. *International Multidisciplinary Conference on Industrial Engineering and Modern Technologies. Far East Con.* Far Eastern Federal University (FEFU). Retrieved from https://www.dvfu.ru/schools/engineering/far_east_con/

Ershov, B. A., & Ashmarov, I. A. (2018). Interaction of the Orthodox Church and the state in Russia at the present stage. *Journal Bulletin Social-Economic and Humanitarian Research, 1*(2),, 19-24. Retrieved from http://bulletensocial.com/index.php/archive.html

Ershov, B. A., Ashmarov, I. A., & Danilchenko, S. (2018). The development of Russian church architecture in the 1990s-2017: the state and prospects. *DataONE.* doi:10.15146/R3FQ16

Rykalov, B. C. (1978). The October Revolution in modern French bourgeois historiography, *History of the USSR, 2,* 209-216.

Semennikova, L. I. (1994). *Russia in the global community of civilizations.* Academic Press. (in Russian)

Shatsillo, K. F. (1961). Foreign capital and naval programs of Russia on the eve of the First World War. *Historical Notes, 69*, 73-100.

Sidorov, A. L. (1960). *The financial position of Russia in the years of the First World War (1914-1917).* Publishing House of the Academy of Sciences of the USSR.

Sidorov, E. Y. (1998). Culture of Peace and Culture of Russia. *Polis (Bologna),* (5), 106–113. (in Russian)

Skvortsova, E. M. (1999). *Theory and history of culture.* Academic Press. (in Russian)

Smetanii, S. I., & Kopotopov, M. V. (2002). History of ferrous metallurgy of Russia. Publishing house "Paleotype".

Soskin, V. L. (2004). Russian Soviet Culture (1917-1927): Essays on Social History. Academic Press. (in Russian)

Stepanov, A. I. (1993). Russia's place in the world on the eve of the first world war. *Questions of History, 1993*(2), 156-163.

Tarnovsky, K. N. (1964). On the sociological study of the capitalist mode of production, *Voprosy Istorii, 1*, 120-132.

Tarnovsky, K. N. (1990). Socio-economic history of Russia. The beginning of the 20th century. Soviet historiography of the mid-1950s-1960s. Academic Press.

The development of culture in Russia in 1992-2012. History (Russia in the second half of the 20th - early 21st centuries). (n.d.). Retrieved from https://foxford.ru/wiki/istoriya/razvitie-kultury-v-rossii-v-1992-2012-gg (in Russian)

The main trends in the development of Russian culture in the 90s. 20th century. (n.d.). Retrieved from https://histerl.ru/kurs_sssp/podrobno/osnovnie_tendencii_razvitia_kulturi.htm (in Russian)

Volobuev, P. V. (1956). Monopoly capitalism in Russia and its features. Academic Press.

Voslensky, M. S. (1991). *Nomenclature: The ruling class of the Soviet Union*. Academic Press. (in Russian)

Ways of Eurasia: Russian intelligentsia and the fate of Russia. (1992). Academic Press. (in Russian)

Zamaraev, E. I. (2016). Results of the cultural policy of Russia in the post-Soviet period. *Humanities. Bulletin of the Financial University, 4*(24). Retrieved from https://cyberleninka.ru/article/n/rezultaty-kulturnoy-politiki-rossii-v-postsovetskiy-period (in Russian)

Zezina, M. R., Koshman, L.V., & Shulgin, V. S. (1990). *History of Russian culture*. Academic Press. (in Russian)

Chapter 6
Soviet Culture in the Years of the Great Patriotic War and the Post-War Period

Igor Asmarov
Voronezh State Institute of Arts, Russia

ABSTRACT

Soviet culture during the Great Patriotic War and the postwar period is conventionally divided into two periods: Soviet culture during the war years 1941-1945; and Soviet culture in the postwar period 1946-1950s. Of course, these stages of the evolution of Soviet culture differ from each other in many respects, as well as in the most important, that is, in their substantive relation. What suffered during the war during the first stage was either restored or rebuilt after the end of the war. Soviet culture during the Great Patriotic War suffered greatly in material and organizational terms. However, at the same time, the culture of the USSR in the years of the war acquired a great deal spiritually and morally. Previously unprecedented patriotism raised the whole country, the entire multinational Soviet people, to fight against the common worst enemy of all progressive humanity - fascism. Soviet culture reflected this rise in patriotism in music, painting, theater and cinema, on stage, in sculpture and architecture, etc. This time was the heyday of the multinational character of the Soviet people, the time of the epochal upsurge of folk culture, folk art, and the consciousness of the masses of the Soviet people.

DOI: 10.4018/978-1-5225-9985-2.ch006

INTRODUCTION

State policy in this period was aimed at fostering patriotism. Therefore, with the beginning of the Great Patriotic War, the main trend in Soviet art was a patriotic theme. Glorification of the heroic past of the Russian people, which began in the pre-war period, greatly intensified.

The heroism and tension of all the spiritual forces of the multinational Soviet people in the war were maximum, which was sung and displayed on movie screens and country scenes of the Soviets. In all of this there was a communist ideology here, but then it was perceived by the working people quite naturally and normally.

Soviet patriotic songs of A. V. Aleksandrov, B. A. Mokrousov, V. P. Solovyov-Sedoi, M. I. Blanter, I. Dunaevsky, the symphony of D. D. Shostakovich and S. Prokofiev and other composers raised morale of Soviet citizens, strengthened their confidence in victory. During the war, many writers, including M.A. Sholokhov, A.A. Surkov, A.P. Gaidar, B.N. Polevoy became military correspondents in the central newspapers, appeared with their works on the radio, Sovinformbureau and TASS. The editors of the front-line newspapers were writers: V.A. Zakrutkin, Yu. P. Herman, A.S. Levada, I.L. Andronikov, S.P. Shchipachev and other well-known figures in Soviet literature.

Campaign leaflets and posters were widely used to mobilize the army and the people to fight the aggressor, expose his propaganda, disintegrate the enemy. The political organs of the fronts, armies and divisions published them. In the newspapers for the first time appeared the "Science of Hatred" by M.A. Sholokhov, "The People are Immortal" by V.S. Grossman.

Famous artists of the theater, cinema and stage created creative teams that went to the front, to hospitals, factory shops and collective farms. At the front, 42,000 creative workers gave 440,000 performances and concerts. Performances of famous artists raised the militant mood, helped to overcome the hardships of the front and rear.

The main content of cinematography in wartime was the heroic struggle of the Soviet people against the aggressor. Documentaries about the heroism and courage of Soviet people were prepared: "All forces to defeat the enemy", "To defend our native Moscow", "Leningrad in the struggle", "The Battle for Our Soviet Ukraine" and others. Feature films, created during the war, told of Communist underground workers, partisans, life in the occupied territory and people who were forcibly taken to Germany (Batyuk, 2005).

In the films, examples of loyal friendship and fidelity were also reflected. Especially popular films were: "Secretary of the District Committee" (1942, directed by IA Pyryev), "Rainbow" (1944, directed by MS Donskoy), "Man No. 217" (1945, directed by M I.Romm), "Two Fighters" (1943, directed by LD Lukov), "Wait for Me" (1943, directed by AB Stolper), "Antosh Rybkin" (1942, director K. K. Yudin), etc. In these and other films, famous actors and actresses were shot: N.M. Uzhviy, E.A. Kuzmina, B.F. Andreev, M. Bernes and others. One of the leading genres remained a comedy that raised the mood and morale of people at the front and in the rear.

In the central newspapers were published publicist articles by A. N. Tolstoy, A. A. Fadeev, M. A. Sholokhov, radio patriotic verses of A. A. Surkov, N. N. Aseev, M. Isakovsky and others and poets. From June 27 in Moscow, and then in other cities, "Windows TASS" - agitational and political posters were posted. The content of the TASS windows was varied: information about the latest developments at the front; calls for vigilance; to strengthening the unity of the front and rear; satirical pamphlets on the enemy, etc. In their creation, the active participation was taken by the poets D. Bednyi, A. A. Aduev, S. I. Kirsanov, A. A. Zharov, graphic artists and cartoonists A. P. Bubnov, N. A. Dolgorukov, A. A. Radakov, MM Cheremnykh. In all, over the years of the war, over 1,200 "Windows TASS" were issued, which were distributed abroad, in the USA, Sweden, India and other countries.

The main themes of artistic and journalistic literature, music, cinema, other art trends were plots from Russia's heroic past, facts of courage, loyalty and devotion to the Motherland of Soviet people who fought the enemy at the front and in the occupied territories.

Soviet culture during the Great Patriotic War was the weapon that helped beat the hated enemy at the front, raising the morale of soldiers and officers. In the rear, it gave strength to accomplish labor feats, strengthened the belief in victory over the enemy.

During the war the state policy of the USSR placed all the achievements of the national culture in the service of the Motherland, protecting it from invaders, achieving victory over the enemy.

The war time required the restructuring of the whole system of cultural institutions, the forms, methods and content of their work. The role of more mass, operative, accessible forms of cultural work has increased: radio, cinema, and print. A lot of work was done to evacuate cultural institutions and cultural treasures to the eastern regions of the country.

Thousands of representatives of art culture - writers, poets, artists, artists, musicians, filmmakers fought on the fronts of the Great Patriotic War, and many of these people died. During the war years, the works of Soviet writers and poets appeared, which became popular among the people: the heads of the novel M.A. Sholokhov "They fought for their Motherland," the poem by A.T. Tvardovsky "Vasily Terkin", verses of K.M. Simonova, A.A. Surkov, M.V. Isakovsky, M.A. Svetlova, N.S. Tikhonov and others. Many songs of the war years were included in the golden fund of Soviet culture, among them "In the dugout" (A. Surkov's words, K. Listov's music), "Dark Night" (V. Agatov's words, N. Bogoslovsky's music), "Evening in the roadstead "(A. Churkin's works, V. Solovyov-Sedov's music)," Nightingales "(A. Fatyanov's words, V. Soloviev-Sedov's music)," Eh, roads" (L. Oshanin's words, music by A. Novikov). In many theaters of the country there were plays of K.M. Simonova "Russian people", A.E. Korneichuk "Front", L.M. Leonova "Invasion", collecting crowded halls (Ryabenko, 2014).

To maintain the morale of the soldiers, front-line brigades of artists, writers, musicians were organized, front-line theaters operated. The actors performed at recruiting stations, in hospitals, at enterprises, directly on the front line. Filmmakers created the films "Alexander Nevsky", "Suvorov", "Schors" and others, inspiring people in a fair fight with the enemy, selfless labor in the rear, inspiring faith in victory. Great contribution to the historical chronicle of the war of documentary filmmakers, who left descendants thousands of kilometers of priceless film material.

Artists participated in a common struggle with the enemy versatile. So, writers and artists V.M. Gusev, S.Ya. Marshak, S.V. Mikhalkov, N.S. Tikhonov and Kukryniksy gave their Stalin Prize for the construction of the tank "Merciless." Artist V.N. Yakhontov built his own aircraft, Vladimir Mayakovsky, at his own expense. There are many such examples in the history of the Great Patriotic War (Leksin, 2015).

The figures of all the directions of the national culture gave their talent, labor and energy to the victory over the enemy. It was a fusion of the military, economic might of our state and the spiritual potential of the people. The victory in the Great Patriotic War was not only military and economic, but also a spiritual victory over the enemy.

The war caused colossal moral and material damage to the Soviet people and the State and the Soviet culture. Millions of Soviet citizens died, tens of millions of people were maimed by fate and health. Hundreds of cities, tens of thousands of villages and villages were destroyed.

Numerous cultural monuments were lost. The fascists destroyed more than 80,000 schools, hundreds of universities, plundered 430 museums, 44,000 houses of culture and libraries, took away from the country many priceless treasures of national culture. All this had a negative impact on the development of artistic culture in the post-war period.

The following characteristics and features of the development of culture in this period can be noted, namely:

- Evacuation of cultural institutions and cultural property;
- The growth of patriotism and the widespread growth of the creative movement of the masses;
- Increase in the production of campaign leaflets and anti-fascist posters;
- Organization of creative teams;
- Organization of front brigades;
- Organization of front theaters;
- Death and destruction, as well as the forced removal by the Nazis of cultural monuments from the USSR.

SOVIET CULTURE IN THE POSTWAR PERIOD

The transition from war to peace created favorable conditions for the development of culture, government spending on which increased significantly.

In the postwar period, much in the development of culture had to start over. During the war years, the number of schools sharply decreased (82,000 schools were destroyed, many higher educational institutions, scientific research institutes, museums and other cultural institutions). However, already in the first postwar five-year plan, much was done to restore and develop the public education system. The most important result of this work was the introduction in the country of universal compulsory seven-year education. Despite the difficulties of the postwar period, the research of scientists gained wide scope. In the country in many branches of science there were scientific schools of global importance.

In the Soviet humanities of this period, new approaches to the study of social consciousness are being developed. This is due to the fact that the Soviet people are beginning to get acquainted with the culture of other countries and to carry out spiritual contacts with all continents.

After the war, domestic culture continued the artistic development of the military theme. A generation of front-line soldiers entered the literature, whose new life experience needed comprehension. The novel by A. Fadeev "Young Guard" and "The Story of a Real Man" by B. Polevoy are created on a documentary basis. One of the first to try to tell the truth about the war V. Nekrasov in the story "In the trenches of Stalingrad". But the hopes of freeing culture from the pressures of official politics and ideology in the post-war years were not destined to be realized. Literature and art were still viewed as a means of educating the masses.

In the art installation was made on masterpieces. Art museums were supposed to exhibit only the highest examples of national art. In the movies, this policy led to a sharp reduction in the number of new films. Historical biographical films, often sketchy and pompous, occupied a significant place on the screen. The most outstanding film production on a historical theme is the film of S. Eisenstein "Ivan the Terrible", finished in 1945 was banned (the ban applied to the second series of the film).

The Soviet theaters were in a difficult situation. The notices of the war years were replaced by half-empty halls. In most theaters, the genre prevailed on the scene. Massive ideological campaigns had a huge negative impact on the development of the entire national culture of the postwar period.

POSTWAR CULTURE

Features of the national culture of the postwar period. The main features of the development of the Soviet culture in this period were:

- The revival of the destroyed centers of culture
- Increased interference of the party-state apparatus in the cultural life of society
- Struggle with bourgeois ideology and cosmopolitanism in culture at the level of state policy
- Administrative intervention in the creative activity of representatives of culture
- Deep deformations in the development of the spiritual life of society.

The development of science and culture in the USSR in the postwar years was combined with a toughening of the struggle against any, even the slightest, deviations from the "tasks of socialist construction".

In 1946, the state budget allocated 3.8 billion rubles for education (in 1940 it was 2.3 billion rubles), in 1950 this amount increased to 5.7 billion rubles. In 1946, the All-Union Committee for Higher Education was transformed into the Ministry of Higher Education of the USSR, in 1950 the Division of Science and Higher Educational Institutions was organized in the Central Committee of the CPSU (b).

In 1946, the Soviet government significantly increased the cost of science. This year the Academy of Sciences of Ukraine, Belarus and Lithuania were restored, established in Kazakhstan, Latvia and Estonia. The second half of the 1940s was the time of the organization of a whole series of scientific research institutes, which later went into the gold fund of Soviet science. Among them were the Institute of Precision Mechanics and Computer Engineering, the Institute of Radio Engineering and Electronics. Institute of Applied Physics, Institute of Atomic Energy and many others. At the same time, there continued to exist and expand special design bureaus that were in the system of the Ministry of Internal Affairs of the USSR.

CONCLUSION

The development of Soviet culture in the years of the Great Patriotic War and the post-war period passed through many ordeals and obstacles. This is a war with a foreign enemy, and the violence of their own party-state power. Nevertheless, the people could not be left without a spiritual and living culture, and it had one that helped restore the country, raise the national economy, and build a new future under the political and economic flag of socialism.

In the second half of the 1940s - early 1950s, the country healed wounds caused by the war. Much work has been done in the field of cultural construction. The network of cultural and educational institutions was restored: museums, theaters, libraries, houses of culture, clubs. Their number has increased significantly compared with the pre-war level.

REFERENCES

Aristarkhov, V. V., & Anisimov, E. A. (2015). *Basics of the state cultural policy*. Moscow, Russia: Ministry of Culture of the Russian Federation. Retrieved from http://www.folkcentr.ru/wp-content/uploads/2017/03/Basic-GKP.pdf

Ashmarov, I. A. (2015). The value and role of theatrical art in the formation of the mentality of Russians. Man in art: in search of national identity. VIII Bolkhovitinovskie reading. In *International Scientific Conference,* (pp. 35-41). Voronezh, Russia: Voronezh State Institute of Arts. (in Russian)

Ashmarov, I. A. (2017). The value of state financial policy for the development of the economy and social sphere. In *Socio-political processes in the modern world: the view of the young: materials of the scientific-practical conference* (pp. 13-19). Voronezh, Russia: Editorial and publishing department of the Voronezh branch of the Russian Presidential Academy of National Economy and Public Administration. (in Russian)

Batyuk, L. I. (2005). *Culture of Russia in the years of the Great Patriotic War* (Dissertation). Retrieved from http://www.dissercat.com/content/kultura-rossii-v-gody-velikoi-otechestvennoi-voiny (in Russian)

Dekanova, M. K. (2008). The formation of the Soviet festive culture in the village in the 1920s. *Bulletin of the Samara State University. Humanitarian Issue, 1,* 20-27.

Dekanova, M. K. (2009). Transformation of the Russian festive culture at the end of the 19th - the first third of the 20th century: the center and the province. dis. Cand. ist sciences. Samara, Russia.

Fomin, V. I. (1996). *Cinema and power: Soviet cinema, 1965-1985: documents, testimonies, reflections*. Moscow, Russia: Materik.

Fomin, V. I. (1998). *Cinema Thaw: Documents and Evidence*. Moscow, Russia: Materik.

Fomin, V. I. (2005). *Cinema in war. Documents and certificates*. Moscow, Russia: Materik.

Fomin, V. I. (2019). *History of Russian cinematography (1941-1968): management, public organizations, repertoire politics, film production, film certification, film distribution, film engineering, foreign relations, personnel training. State Central Cinema Museum, Russian Cinematographers Union*. Moscow: Canon Plus.

Komissarov, S. S. (2011). Politics in the sphere of culture: the vector of spiritual revival of the national civilization. *Bulletin of Moscow State University of Culture and Art, 1*. Retrieved from https://cyberleninka.ru/article/n/politika-v-sfere-kultury-vektor-duhovnogo-vozrozhdeniya-otechestvennoy-tsivilizatsii

Leksin, V. N. (2015). The Great Culture of the Great War. *Outlines of Global Transformations: Politics, Economics, Law, 3*(41). Retrieved from https://cyberleninka.ru/article/n/velikaya-kultura-velikoy-voyny (in Russian)

Plaggenborg, S. (2000). Revolution and culture. In *Cultural landmarks in the period between the October Revolution and the era of Stalinism* (pp. 287-321). Saint Petersburg, Russia: Academic Press.

Rolf, M. (2009). Soviet mass holidays. Moscow, Russia: ROSSPEN.

Ryabenko, V. (2014). *Soviet culture in the years of the Great Patriotic War and in the post-war period.* Retrieved from https://magref.ru/sovetskaya-kultura-v-godyi-velikoy-otechestvennoy-voynyi-i-v-poslevoennyiy-period (in Russian)

Sazhina, A. I. (2015). The state policy of the Soviet government in the field of education and enlightenment of the adult population in 1917-1927. Astrakhan, Russia: Academic Press.

Stradina, E. A. (2007). State policy of Russia in the field of culture in the context of the reform of the political system. Yaroslavl, Russia: Academic Press.

Suanova, R. E. (2012). State policy in the field of culture in 1917-1941. (on materials of North Ossetia). Vladikavkaz, Russia: Academic Press.

Sviridov, E. G. (2014). State policy of the USSR in the sphere of festive culture (20s-40s). *The Times of Science, 2.* Retrieved from https://cyberleninka.ru/article/n/gosudarstvennaya-politika-sssr-v-sfere-prazdnichnoy-kultury-20-40-e-gg

The project. (2004, May 16). *Fundamentals of the state cultural policy.* Retrieved from https://rg.ru/2014/05/15/osnovi-dok.html

Yeleskina, O. V. (2005). State policy in the field of culture. Kemerovo, Russia: Academic Press.

Zakovich, N. M., Kosuha, P. I., & Perunov, V. A. (1986). Socialist rites. Kiev, Ukraine: Academic Press.

Zakovich, N. M., Zots, V. A. (1980). Holidays and rituals as an element of Soviet culture. *Questions of Scientific Atheism,* (26), 165-177.

Chapter 7
The Socio-Cultural Process in the USSR in 1950-1980

Igor Asmarov
Voronezh State Institute of Arts, Russia

ABSTRACT

These four decades gave the USSR new discoveries in the sphere of cultural creativity and the growth of the military and economic power of the country, including the Soviet Union republics of the USSR. The social and cultural process in the USSR in 1950-1980 proceeded under the strong influence of ideology and the ideological and political conjuncture. Nevertheless, creative thought in the sphere of culture and art in the USSR was alive and even fruitfully developed. The peculiarities of the culture of the USSR of this period consisted in the struggle of the government against deviations from the "tasks of social construction". The pressure and control from the party were so great that they oppressed the freedom of artists and science. Mass discussions in various branches of science of this time had a negative effect on their participants. The development of culture in the 1960-80s was extremely controversial. Despite the fact that the funds for the development of culture constantly increased, the achievements in culture did not correspond to the financial costs. During this period, the leadership of the USSR began to pay great attention to public education and science.

DOI: 10.4018/978-1-5225-9985-2.ch007

INTRODUCTION

The war and repression of the 1930s dealt a heavy blow to the intelligentsia, so in the 1940s and early 1950s the Soviet Union had a huge deficit of specialists with higher and secondary education. The difficulties faced by the sphere of education in the USSR were solved by lowering the educational level. Although teachers and university professors, like all researchers, significantly increased their salaries and provided a number of benefits, their preparation was lower even compared to the 1930s. Most school teachers were trained in short-term courses or in teacher training institutes for a shorter program.

Despite all this, the country switched to universal seven-year education. The lowering of the general educational level subsequently led to crisis phenomena in the science and economy of the Soviet state, but at that time it gave a quick effect, created the illusion of accelerated scientific and technological development of society. In the 1940s and early 1950s, Soviet science and technology achieved a number of successes, primarily in the fields of physics, chemistry, and precision mechanics, but they were mostly aimed at military needs.

In 1949, the atomic bomb was tested in the USSR, intensive research was carried out in the field of chemical and bacteriological weapons.

At the same time, the branches of science that did not have a direct relationship to defense were subjected to harsh pressure and even bans.

If in the development of exact and natural sciences the interference and dictatorship of the party-state apparatus were a brake, then for the humanities they became a catastrophe. For the first post-war decade, in the humanities, not a single serious achievement has emerged, and in the field of literature and art - not a single outstanding work.

The campaign to combat cosmopolitanism, which unfolded in the late 1940s and early 1950s, adversely affected the development of science, literature and art.

Its aim was to denigrate all non-Soviet, non-socialist, to put a barrier between the Soviet people and the achievements of the culture of Western countries. As a result of this campaign, many figures of science and art were repressed, dismissed from their posts and even imprisoned and exiled. The Party and the government openly and actively interfered in the work of writers and artists, which led to a decline in the artistic and ideological level, the formation of mediocre, embellishing the Soviet reality of art.

Soviet composers, writers and poets: D. Shostakovich, S. Prokofiev, A. Khachaturyan, N. Myaskovsky, A. Akhmatova, M. Zoshchenko and others, whose work was referred to the "anti-popular" trend, were persecuted.

All this led to a sharp reduction in the number of new films, plays and art works, to the conscious breakdown of the great Russian artistic tradition of the 19th and early 20th centuries.

The culture in the post-war period was heavily influenced by state power. The same influence, however, took place in other periods of Russian history. The war caused considerable damage to the domestic culture, its material base. Thousands of schools, hundreds of universities and museums were destroyed, tens of thousands of books burned or taken out of the country. Many talented scientists, writers, and artists have not returned from the front. The output of specialists in higher education institutions has decreased.

In difficult conditions of the post-war period, the state sought funds for the development of science, public education, and art. The revival of the destroyed centers of culture began immediately after the expulsion of the enemy from the occupied territories and continued in subsequent years.

A characteristic feature of the development of culture in the postwar years was the increased intervention of the party-state apparatus in the cultural life of society. The sphere of ideology was viewed as an ideological front, where the main blow should be directed against the remnants of bourgeois views and adulation of the culture of the bourgeois West, against the departure from Marxism in science, literature and art.

The requirements for the work of the creative intelligentsia were reflected in the decisions of the Central Committee of the Party of the second half of the 1940s on questions of literature and art. Among the first there was a resolution "On the journals" Zvezda "and" Leningrad "(1946). The reason for it was the publication in the magazine "Murzilka" of Mikhail Zoshchenko's story "The Adventures of a Monkey", reprinted later by the literary magazine Zvezda. A political evaluation of M. Zoshchenko's children's story was given at a meeting of the Orgburo of the Central Committee of the Party, attended by I. V. Stalin, A.A. Zhdanov, secretary of the Central Committee on ideology, other ideological workers, as well as writers. The stories, stories and poems of a number of authors were recognized as incompatible with the socialist worldview. Mikhail Zoshchenko was accused of lack of ideology, vulgarity and apoliticality. The decree and explanatory publications contained political accusations and insults against A.A. Akhmatova, M.M. Zoshchenko and other Soviet writers.

One-sided, unjustifiably sharp assessment of the work of a group of talented playwrights and composers, theater and cinema figures contained the resolutions of the Central Committee of the Party “On the repertoire of dramatic theaters”, “On the film “Big Life”, “On the Great Friendship” V. Muradeli and others. These decisions severely affected the creative destinies of individual cultural figures, the subsequent development of literature and art.

At the turn of the 1940s and 1950s, the Party Central Committee organized discussions on philosophy, political economy and linguistics. In addition to the representatives of science, the leaders of the party and the state took part in them. Thus, in a discussion organized to discuss the book of G.F. Aleksandrov on the history of Western European philosophy, took part A.A. Zhdanov. He accused the author of the textbook of bowing to bourgeois Western philosophy, urging Soviet scientists “to lead the struggle against the corrupt and vile bourgeois ideology”.

At the end of the 1940s, cosmopolitans announced the representatives of science, literature and art, whose work saw “worshiping everything Western”. Especially strongly this campaign has affected a historical science. Many famous Soviet scientists (I. I. Mints, I. M. Razgon, etc.) were accused of distorting the history of Soviet society. The writings of these authors were charged with belittling the role of the USSR in the world historical process, undermining the role of the Russian people and the Russian working class in the victory of the October Revolution and the Civil War, in building a socialist society. The struggle against cosmopolitanism was accompanied by “elaborations” and administrative measures against well-known researchers. It led to the fact that the concepts of historical development that had developed in the 1930s-1940s remained intact for many years to come. The slightest deviations in the works of scientists from the prevailing views, their attempt to take a new look at scientific questions were considered as a violation of the principle of partisanship in science.

Administrative interference in the creative activity of representatives of culture, the struggle against “bourgeois ideology,” political assessments of artistic creativity and scientific work during the cult of Stalin’s personality caused profound deformations in the development of the spiritual life of society (Ashmarov, 2017).

"THAW" («OTTEPEL») AND THE ARTISTIC INTELLIGENTSIA

During the Khrushchev "thaw" ideological influence on the creative work of the artistic intelligentsia was significantly weakened. In 1958, the Central Committee of the CPSU adopted a resolution "On the correction of errors in the evaluation of the operas "Great Friendship","Bogdan Khmelnitsky","With all my heart". Many cultural figures were rehabilitated - victims of political repression.

Khrushchev's thaw is an unofficial designation of a period in the history of the USSR after the death of Stalin, which lasted about ten years (mid-1950s-mid-1960s).

This period was characterized in the internal political life of the USSR by condemning the cult of Stalin's personality and the repressions of the 1930s, the release of political prisoners, and the liquidation of the GULAG. At this time, there was a weakening of totalitarian power, the appearance of some freedom of speech, the relative liberalization of political and public life, openness to the Western world, greater freedom of creative activity. The name is associated with the presence of Nikita Khrushchev (1955-1964) as the first secretary of the CPSU Central Committee. The name is associated with the presence of Nikita Khrushchev (1955-1964) as the first secretary of the CPSU Central Committee. The very word "thaw" is associated with the story of the same name by Ilya Ehrenburg.

"THAW" («OTTEPEL») IN ART

During the period of de-Stalinization, censorship was noticeably weakened, primarily in literature, cinema and other types of art, where more critical coverage of reality became possible. "The first poetic bestseller" "thaw" was a collection of poems by Leonid Martynov (Poems, M., Young Guard, 1955). The main platform of supporters of the "thaw" was the literary magazine "New World". Some works of this period gained fame abroad, including the novel by Vladimir Dudintsev "Not by bread alone" and Alexander Solzhenitsyn's novel One Day of Ivan Denisovich. In 1957, a novel by Boris Pasternak, Doctor Zhivago, was published in Milan. Other significant representatives of the "thaw" period were writers and poets Viktor Astafyev, Vladimir Tendryakov, Bella Akhmadulina, Robert Rozhdestvensky, Andrei Voznesensky, Yevgeny Yevtushenko.

There was a sharp increase in the production of motion pictures. Grigory Chukhrai was the first in the cinema to touch upon de-Stalinization and the "thaw" in the film "Clear Sky" (1963). The main filmmakers of this period are Marlen Khutsiev, Mikhail Romm, Georgy Danelia, Eldar Ryazanov, Leonid Gaidai. An important cultural event was the films "Carnival Night", "Zastava Ilyicha", "Spring on Zarechnaya Street", "Idiot", "I walk around Moscow", "Amphibian Man", "Come Tomorrow ...", "Welcome" or No Trespassing "and others.

The revival of the spiritual life of society was facilitated by the emergence of new creative unions. The Union of Writers of the RSFSR, the Union of Artists of the RSFSR, the Union of Cinematographers of the USSR were formed. There were not published previously literary and socio-political magazines "Moscow", "Neva", "Foreign Literature", "Youth", etc. In the capital of the USSR was opened a new drama theater "Contemporary", the basis of the troupe were graduates of the school-studio MKhAT. Literary evenings of famous writers and poets were held (Ashmarov, 2015).

In the late 1950s and early 1960s, several meetings of party and state leaders took place with representatives of the artistic intelligentsia. N. S. Khrushchev and secretary of the Central Committee on the ideology of L. F. Ilyichev accepted participation in them.

Relations between the head of state and the figures of literature and art were not easy to form. Work to restore the rule of law, on the rehabilitation of innocent convicts brought N. S. Khrushchev's wide popularity. However, his attempts to interfere in the creative laboratory of cultural workers, incompetence and categorical in the assessments of their creativity led to the loss of their authority. A certain role in this was played by the persecution of the talented writer and poet B.L. Pasternak. In 1958, for the novel "Doctor Zhivago", banned for publication in the USSR and published abroad, B.L. Pasternak was awarded the Nobel Prize in Literature. In the same year, he was expelled from the Union of Writers of the USSR and forced to abandon the Nobel Prize.

One of the consequences of the liberalization of the foreign policy was the deepening of international ties among cultural figures. Representatives of science and art, university professors were sent for training to different countries of the world. The exchange of information between scientific research institutes, their mutual cooperation in solving important problems of science and technology were expanded. In the USSR, exhibitions were organized from the largest art galleries of the world. There were performances of the best foreign theater and music groups. In Moscow, the first International

Competition of Musicians and Performers by P. I. Tchaikovsky. One of his laureates was pianist Van Cliburn from the USA.

POST-WAR IDEOLOGICAL CAMPAIGNS

On the whole, the postwar ideological and political situation in the country was not quite favorable for the development of culture and science. Distribution received dogmatism, quotation. The criterion of truth became the statements of leaders.

The isolationist policies of the Soviet leadership were reinforced by a broad ideological campaign to fight slander against the West. Pages of newspapers and magazines filled out articles praising everything domestic, Russian and Soviet. Journalists have argued Russian championship in almost all scientific and technical discoveries.

The campaign against pangs touched artistic life. The visual art of the West, beginning with the Impressionists, was declared entirely decadent. In 1948, the Museum of New Western Art was closed.

Major discoveries by foreign scientists in the field of quantum mechanics and cybernetics were declared hostile to materialism. The genetics and molecular biology that were recognized as false were particularly affected, and their research has almost ceased. At the session of the All-Union Academy of Agricultural Sciences (All-Russian Academy of Agricultural Sciences) in August 1948 a group of T. Lysenko took a monopoly position in the field of agrobiology, supported by the country's leadership. As a result, Soviet biology was severely damaged by a typically domestic invention, Lysenkoism, and was thrown back in its research many years ago.

In 1947, there was a discussion on philosophy, in 1950 - on linguistics, in 1951 - on political economy. In the first discussion, the party was represented by a member of the Political Bureau of the Central Committee, which was concerned with ideology, A. A. Zhdanov, in the other two - I. V. Stalin. Their participation excluded the possibility of a free discussion of problems, and speeches were perceived as guidelines. It should be noted that even in Lenin's legacies were made bills. So, in the fourth edition of the works of V. I. Lenin did not include the work "Letter to the Congress", "On giving legislative functions to the State Planning Committee" and "On the question of nationalities or on" autonomization ", which did not meet the official ideological views and could undermine the prestige of the leaders of the Soviet state.

A typical phenomenon of the end of the 1940s was the ideological campaigns in scientific, university and creative teams that created a nervous atmosphere, and the campaign to combat formalism and cosmopolitanism took a large scale.

In 1948, the first All-Union Congress of Soviet Composers and a three-day meeting of Soviet music figures in the Party Central Committee were held. They manifested a desire to artificially divide composers into realists and formalists. Moreover, D. D. Shostakovich, S. S. Prokofiev, N. Ya. Myaskovsky, V. Ya. Shebalin, A. I. Khachaturian were accused of formalism.

The events of 1948 had a negative impact on the development of professional pop-orchestra (jazz) L. Utesov and E. Rosner were forced to change their orientation.

In the years 1946-1948 in a number of resolutions of the Central Committee of the CPSU (b) ("On the magazines Zvezda" and "Leningrad", "On the repertoire of dramatic theaters and measures to improve it", "On the film "Big Life","On the Opera "The Great Friendship" V. Muradeli") cultural figures were accused of apoliticality, unprincipledness, propaganda of bourgeois ideology. These documents contained offensive assessments of A. A. Akhmatova, M. M. Zoshchenko, D. D. Shostakovich, V. I. Muradeli

In 1946, famous cultural figures such as directors S. Eisenstein, V. I. Pudovkin, G. M. Kozintsev, composers S. S. Prokofyev, D. D. Shostakovich, were criticized and persecuted for incompatibility with general standards. A. I. Khachaturian, N. Ya. Myaskovsky.

The USSR Academy of Arts, created in 1948 and headed by A. M. Gerasimov, was actively involved in the fight against "formalism". The offensive on formalism turned the talented masters A. Osmerkin, R. Falk out of the artistic life, leaving heavy traces in the creative fate of S. Gerasimov, P. Corin, M. Saryan.

The Great Patriotic War and the victory over fascist Germany had a significant effect on the self-consciousness of our people. The self-esteem, independence in the decision of the important vital problems was strengthened. People have hopes for positive changes in the life of society, its democratization. However, these trends contradicted the foundations of the totalitarian regime.

After the war, ideological pressure on culture increased. Party intervention in the sphere of artistic culture was growing. The ideological work of the party was subordinated to the preservation and strengthening of the administrative-command system. The personality cult of Stalin has grown to phenomenal proportions. The image of the "leader of all times and peoples," the image of a prosperous state, its happy citizens, simplified ideas about the "bright future" overwhelmed the pages of newspapers, magazines, books, viewed from art canvases, from cinema screens, etc. Restriction of information, subjects and the content of artistic creativity adversely affected the development of artistic culture.

Party organs openly interfered in the affairs of literature and art, making in most cases decisions that had a detrimental effect on the development of artistic creation. In 1946-1950 resolutions of the Central Committee of the CPSU(b) "On the magazines Zvezda" and "Leningrad", "On the repertoire of drama theaters and measures for its improvement", "On the film" Big Life ", on the opera" Great Friendship "by V. Muradeli were adopted. These resolutions were aimed at tightening ideological regulation in guiding the artistic life of the country, increasing party pressure on all aspects of the creative process.

In 1949-1950 a campaign against cosmopolitanism was launched in the country, during which a number of cultural representatives were attacked, especially those of Jewish nationality.

All this adversely affected the state of artistic culture, caused the appearance of a mass of faceless, varnishing works that flooded Soviet art. But, fortunately, which is natural for any time, artistic life was not exhausted only by this. Time puts everything in its place. All superficial has gone, and true art continued to live. The works of L. M. Leonova, K. G. Paustovsky, K. A. Fedina, A. A. Akhmatova, M. M. Zoshchenko, like the works of our talented composers S. S. Prokofieva, D. D. Shostakovich, N. Ya. Myaskovsky, V. Ya. Shebalina, A. I. Khachaturian, artists P. P. Konchalovsky, P. D. Korina, V. A. Favorsky, filmmakers S. M. Eisenstein, A. P. Dovzhenko, V. I. Pudovkina and many others, whose work has enriched the domestic and world culture.

After the war a large group of talented youth came to literature. These were people who passed through the formidable front-line roads. They knew the war not by hearsay, and their works were distinguished by the harsh truth of life. Their work was called "literature lieutenants." Among them are writers G. Ya. Baklanov ("Spits of the Earth", "The Dead Shame Is Not Imut"), Yu. V. Bondarev ("The battalions are asking for fire", "Hot snow"), V. P. Nekrasov ("In the trenches of Stalingrad"), poets N. K. Starshinov, D. S. Samoilov, S. S. Narovchat, E. M. Vinokurov, M. K. Lukonin, S. P. Gudzenko.

On the situation in literature at the Second All-Union Congress of Soviet Writers in 1954, M. Sholokhov said that the gray flow of colorless works that floods the book market in recent years remains a disaster. The stories about the conflict between the innovator and the conservative, about the transformation of a backward collective farm into a front line, were commonplace. The image of the arrogant director, who is being re-educated by the new progressive leader, who takes the team out of difficulties, is the set of types and level of understanding of social problems.

Ideological propaganda took on an increasingly chauvinistic and anti-Semitic character. In January 1949, a campaign began against "rootless cosmopolitans", which resulted in destructive interference in the fate of a number of scientists, teachers, literary and artistic workers. Most of those accused of cosmopolitanism turned out to be Jews. The fight against cosmopolitanism acquired a particularly ominous meaning against the background of other events of that time: in December 1948, the Jewish Anti-Fascist Committee was dissolved, and its activists were arrested; Jewish cultural institutions were shutting down - theaters, schools, newspapers. This campaign reached its apogee in the last months of Stalin's life when a group of prominent Jewish doctors who were working in the Kremlin hospital and accused of premeditated murder of high-ranking patients were arrested.

Ideological campaigns, the constant search for enemies and their revelations maintained an atmosphere of fear in society.

After the death of Stalin in 1953, the features of totalitarianism continued to exist in cultural policy for a long time. This does not mean that the formation and consolidation of the personality cult is connected with the absence of dissent in the artistic culture of the Soviet period.

Recently, the "Untimely Thoughts" by M. Gorky, "Cursed Days" by I. Bunin, the diaries of M. Prishvin and I. Pavlov have become widely known to the reading public. The protest against spiritual oppression sounds in the works of E. Zamyatin, A. Platonov, M. Bulgakov, the poets N. Klyuev, S. Klychkov, O. Mandelstam.

Time made its selection. Many of the works noted in those years by the Stalin Prize are not remembered now. But remained in the Soviet literature "Golden Carriage" L. M. Leonov, "The Far Years" by K. G. Paustovsky, "The First Joys" and "The Unusual Summer" by K. A. Fedina, "Star" E. G. Kazakevich. In the classics of Soviet cinema entered "Young Guard" SA. Gerasimov and "feat scout" B. V. Barnet.

SOVIET CULTURE IN THE PERIOD OF "THAW" («OTTEPEL») AND "STAGNATION" («ZASTOY»)

"Thaw" in the Soviet culture. The reforms that began after Stalin's death created more favorable conditions for the development of culture. Exposing the personality cult at the 20th Party Congress in 1956, returning hundreds of thousands of repressed people from prisons and exile, including representatives of the creative intelligentsia, weakening the censorship press, developing ties with foreign countries - all this expanded the spectrum of freedom, caused the population, especially the young, Utopian dreams of a better life. The combination of all these completely unique circumstances led to the movement of the sixties.

The time from the mid-1950s to the mid-1960s (from the appearance in 1954 of the story of I. Ehrenburg with the name "Thaw" and until the discovery of the process over A. Sinyavsky and U. Daniel in February 1966) entered the history of the USSR under the name "thaw", although the inertia of the processes unfolding at that time made itself felt until the early 70s.

The concept of "thaw" in the socio-cultural terms had two meanings:

1. **Symbolic:** Thaw in culture preceded and contributed to thaw in other spheres of public life;
2. **Real:** The weakening of the influence of the total regime on the individual process of artistic creativity.

The era of change in Soviet society coincided with a global socio-cultural turn. In the second half of the 1960s, the youth movement became active, opposing itself to the traditional forms of spirituality. For the first time, the historical results of the 20th century are subjected to a deep philosophical understanding and a new artistic interpretation. The problem of the responsibility of "fathers" for the catastrophes of the century more and more often rises, the fatal question of the relationship between "fathers and children" begins to sound in full force.

In Soviet society, the 20th CPSU Congress (February 1956), perceived by public opinion as a cleansing storm, became the boundary of sociocultural changes. The process of spiritual renewal in Soviet society began with a discussion of the responsibility of the "fathers" for departing from the ideals of the October revolution, which became the criterion for measuring the country's historical past, as well as the moral position of the individual.

Thus, the opposition of two social forces came into force: the supporters of renewal, called anti-Stalinists, and their opponents - the Stalinists.

An attempt to answer these questions from different historical and cultural positions (values) led to a split of the creative intelligentsia into traditionalists (oriented towards the traditional values of Soviet culture) and neoavant-garde (adhering to the antisocialist orientation of artistic creativity based on bourgeois-liberal values of postmodernism, into the division of art into elite and mass with the idea of their diffusion).

In fiction, the contradictions within the framework of traditionalism are reflected in the opposition of the conservatives (F. Kochetov - the magazines "October", "Neva", "Literature and Life" and the adjacent magazines "Moscow", "Our Contemporary" and "Young Guard") and Democrats (A. Tvardovsky - magazines "New World", "Youth"). The journal "New World", the editor-in-chief of which was A. T. Tvardovsky, has a special role in the spiritual culture of this time. He opened for the reader the names of many great masters, namely, "One Day of Ivan Denisovich" by A. Solzhenitsyn was published in it.

The plays of V. Rozov, the books of V. Aksenov and A. Gladilin, the poems of E. Evtushenko and A. Voznesensky, the movie of M. Hutsiev's "Zastava Ilyich" played a major role in consolidating the ideology of "thawing". The truth about Stalinism was carried by the works of A. Solzhenitsyn, E. Ginzburg, V. Shalamov and many others.

The activities of the theater groups "Sovremennik" and "Taganka" became a kind of centers of dissent. Their performances, always perceived with a certain subtext, were a kind of protest against the advancing neo-Stalinism.

Art exhibitions of Moscow neo-avant-gardists and literary "samizdat" of the late 50s meant the appearance of values that decried the canons of socialist realism.

Samizdat appeared in the late 1950s. This name was given to typewritten journals, created in an environment of creative youth, opposed to the realities of Soviet reality. The samizdat included works by Soviet authors, for one reason or another, rejected by publishers, as well as the literature of emigrants, and poetry collections of the beginning of the century. Hand went and manuscripts of detectives. The beginning of the "thawing" samizdat was put on the lists of Tvardovsky's poem "Terkin in the Other World", written in 1954, but not allowed for publication and trapped in samizdat against the will of the author. The first samizdat magazine "Syntax", founded by the young poet A. Ginzburg, published the forbidden works of V. Nekrasov, B. Okudzhava, V.

Shalamov, B. Akhmadulina. After Ginzburg was arrested in 1960, the first dissidents picked up the samizdat baton (Vladimir Bukovsky and others).

The sociocultural origins of anti-socialist art had their own basis. The example of B. Pasternak's worldview is characteristic in this sense (M. Gorky considered him the best poet of socialist realism in the 30s), who published the novel Doctor Zhivago in the West, where the author critically rethinks the events of the October Revolution. The expulsion of Pasternak from the Writers' Union drew a line in the relationship between the authorities and the artistic intelligentsia.

Cultural policy in the period of "thaw". N. Khrushchev clearly formulated the task and role of the intelligentsia in public life: to reflect the growing importance of the party in communist construction and to be its "machine gunners". The control over the activities of the artistic intelligentsia was carried out through the "orientation" meetings of the country's leaders with leading cultural figures. N. S. Khrushchev, Minister of Culture E. A. Furtseva, the main ideologist of the party M. A. Suslov was not always able to make a qualified decision regarding the artistic value of the works criticized by them. This led to unjustified attacks on cultural figures. Khrushchev sharply spoke out against the poet A. A. Voznesensky, whose poems differ in complicated figurativeness and rhythm, filmmakers M. M. Khutsiev, author of the films "Spring on Zarechnaya Street" and "Two Fedor", M. I. Romm, staged in 1962, the feature film "Nine Days of One Year."

In December 1962, during a visit to the exhibition of young artists in the Manezh, Khrushchev arranged the dressing for "formalists" and "abstractionists", among whom was sculptor Ernst Unknown. All this created a nervous situation among the creative workers, contributed to the growth of distrust of the party's cultural policy.

The time of the Khrushchev "thaw" directly and indirectly separated and disoriented the creative intelligentsia: some overestimated the nature of superficial changes, others failed to see their "secretive overtones" (outside influence), others could not already express the fundamental interests of the victorious people, the fourth were only capable of propaganda of interests of the party-state apparatus. All this, ultimately, caused inadequate reality of art works, dominated by the ideals of democratic socialism.

On the whole, the "thaw" turned out to be not only short-lived, but also rather superficial, it did not create guarantees against a return to the Stalinist practice. The warming was not sustainable, ideological indulgence was replaced by rude administrative intervention, and by the mid-1960s the thaw had disappeared, but its value went beyond the brief bursts of cultural life. In those years, the first and decisive step was taken in overcoming Stalinism, the return of the cultural heritage of emigration, the restoration of cultural continuity and international cultural exchange began. In the years of the "thaw" the "Sixties", a generation of intelligentsia, was formed, which later played an important role in restructuring. The emergence of alternative sources of information — samizdat, broadcasts of foreign radio stations — had major implications for public consciousness.

General characteristics of the Soviet culture of the period of "stagnation". For more than twenty years in Soviet history there was an era of "stagnation", which in the field of culture was characterized by contradictory trends. On the one hand, the fruitful development of all spheres of scientific and artistic activity continued, thanks to state funding, the material base of culture was strengthened. On the other hand, the ideological control of the country's leadership over the work of writers, poets, artists and composers has increased.

During this long period of time, serious changes have occurred in all areas of social life. Thanks to scientific, technical and informational progress, there was a split and reorientation of the public consciousness, especially among young people, towards the traditional values of Russian culture and towards Western patterns of life.

There was disunity, which was observed among the creative intelligentsia, acquired quite clear outlines of the confrontation between the two cultures - officially nomenklatura (part of the creative elite merged with the higher echelons of power) and the national-democratic autonomies and areas).

It should be noted the evolution of the forms of this confrontation - from a sharp rejection to the establishment of a certain mutual agreement and interaction, which was dictated by the vital need to change the orientation of internal and external development. Thus, the logic of the development of the subject of display of reality by the official culture was associated with an attempt to maintain its dominant position in the public consciousness, which caused a transition from the obvious "varnishing" of the phenomena of the surrounding life to the traditions of neo-Stalinism, thereby reviving the spiritual values of Russian culture historical themes (for example, the films "War and Peace" and "Andrei Rublev," directed by S. Bondarchuk and A. Tarkovsky).

An essential feature of the sociocultural model of "stagnation" was the beginning of the revival of national traditions "from below" and not "from above." In other words, the process of "cleansing" the core of Russian culture occurs through the development of urban culture, objectively aimed at the revival of traditional rituals and values, and through the artistic creativity of the “village people” (F. Abramova, V. Belova, B. Mozhaeva, V. Shushkina, etc.), which showed the originality and vitality of the Russian village.

The process of growth of contradictions, caused by the formation of national cultures both in Great Russian and in each union republic (territory, region, etc.), prepared the necessary groundwork for the sociocultural policy of “Perestroika”.

The cultural policy of the period of “stagnation”. With the advent of the new political leadership (L. I. Brezhnev), the process of disengagement of the intelligentsia accelerated. An important turning point was the arrest in 1965 of the writers A. Sinyavsky and Y. Daniel on charges of anti-Soviet activities. This activity was reduced to the publication under pseudonyms in the West of several literary works. In February 1966 a trial took place. This was the first open political process after Stalin’s death, and he made a depressing impression on his contemporaries: writers were tried for literary works, and, despite pressure, they did not admit their guilt.

In 1970, the last stronghold of the liberal intelligentsia was liquidated. With the resignation of A. Tvardovsky from the post of editor-in-chief of the New World, the magazine lost its role as an organ of democratic forces. Tvardovsky’s forced departure from the “New World” reflected the intensification of conservative tendencies in the management of cultural life. In subsequent years, these trends intensified.

Externally democratic forms of cultural management could not overshadow the true state of affairs. During these years, congresses of teachers, workers of higher schools, creative intelligentsia, and conferences of social scientists regularly convened. However, they gradually turned into ceremonial events held according to a previously agreed scenario.

The administrative-bureaucratic system that emerged in the late 1920s - early 1930s has taken deep roots. Attempts to overcome the consequences of the Stalin personality cult did not affect the foundations of this system, but only gave it a certain democratic appearance. Strengthening of administrative pressure can be traced in various spheres of cultural life. Difficult, sometimes intolerable conditions were created for the work of educators and innovators, the works or scientific works of authors who held high posts turned out to be beyond criticism. The number of talented works grew that did not fit into the established canons and therefore did not reach the reader or the viewer. Political unreliability was reason enough that a scientist, writer or artist was deprived of the opportunity to engage in creative work.

Some artists have left their homeland due to unbearable working conditions. All this led to the squandering of the intellectual and creative forces of Soviet society, destroying the fate of people. The names of forced emigrants were deleted from Soviet culture, their books were removed from libraries. Tacit bans have become the norm.

In order to regulate the subject of artistic works, a system of state orders was introduced from the mid-1970s, primarily in the field of cinematography. The influence of the censorship press has increased. The concept of a shelf film, shot but not allowed on the screen due to "ideological inconsistency" or the presence of elements of formalism, was born. The same practice extended to the organization of art exhibitions, theatrical performances, the performance of musical works. The acquaintance of the Soviet public with samples of the artistic culture of the countries of Eastern Europe was limited.

In Soviet art, avant-garde directions were forbidden or hushed up; for example, the musical works of A. G. Schnittke were not performed. The works of bard poets B. Sh. Okudzhava, A. A. Galich, V. S. Vysotsky.

The theme of the crimes of Stalinism was considered exhausted, since the party allegedly overcame the "consequences of the cult of personality." In the 1970s, Stalin began to reappear in books and films about the war in the form of a wise commander.

The ideological and organizational problems of cultural life were aggravated by material difficulties.

At the same time, the dissident movement is acquiring more and more active forms.

Dissidence and diversity of its currents. The pressure of the ideological press on the creative intelligentsia was not an arbitrary phenomenon on the part of the authorities, rather a response to the growth of oppositional attitudes in society, expressed in the dissident movement. His birth is often associated with a demonstration on Pushkinskaya Square on December 5, 1965 and a collective written appeal to the authorities with a request to reconsider the court decision and release the writers A. Sinyavsky and Y. Daniel to freedom, as well as an open appearance on Red Square in Moscow on August 25, 1968 Years of eight people protesting against the introduction of Soviet troops in Czechoslovakia.

The growth of political discontent was observed in a number of universities in the country (Tartu, Leningrad), the Institute of Economics of the Siberian Branch of the USSR Academy of Sciences. Its spread was facilitated by the arrests of writers. The trials of them were often indicative in nature; charges were brought under article 70 of the Criminal Code for "agitation or propaganda conducted with the aim of undermining or weakening Soviet power". Following Sinyavsky and Daniel were followed by the arrests of A.

Ginzburg, who compiled the White Book of protests against the first trial of 1966, P. Litvinov, Y. Galanskov, the founders of the samizdat magazine Fenix, A. Marchenko, the author of the first book about the Khrushchev camps ("My testimony"). Since April 1968, the dissident movement began to publish the Chronicle of Current Events, which went underground and informed about all the protests that had taken place.

At the end of the 1960s, the main trends of dissidents united in the "Democratic Movement", represented by three directions: "genuine Marxism-Leninism" (leaders are brothers Roy and Zhores Medvedev), liberalism represented by A. D. Sakharov and traditionalism protected by A. I. Solzhenitsyn.

The Medvedev program advocated a return to the sources of Marxism-Leninism, not distorted by the Stalinist ideology, A. D. Sakharov advocated the introduction of Western-style democracy while maintaining public ownership in the country, A. I. Solzhenitsyn based the ideals of Christian morality and the monarchical political system on the basis of the update. The "democratic movement" did not have a wide resonance in the country, however, its real recognition was gained abroad, primarily thanks to the authority of A. D. Sakharova and A. I. Solzhenitsyn.

Art culture of the period of "stagnation". Despite all the difficulties and contradictions, the literary and artistic life of the 1970s was notable for its diversity and richness. The ideals of humanism and democracy continued to live in literature and art, and the truth about the present and past of Soviet society sounded.

Highly artistic works about the Great Patriotic War were created (Yu. V. Bondarev "Hot Snow", B. L. Vasilyev "And the Dawns Here are Quiet ..." and "Not Listed", K. D. Vorobyov "Killed near Moscow The artistic works of those years not only more boldly revealed the conflicts and events of the past war, but also focused their attention on the fate of a single person in a war.

Acute social problems, and above all the Soviet countryside, were raised by writers V. G. Rasputin (the stories "Deadline", "Live and Remember" and "Farewell to Mother"); V. A. Soloukhin (Vladimirsky Prosley); V. P. Astafyev (Theft and Tsar-Ryba); F. A. Abramov (Trilogy of Pryazlina and The House), V. I. Belov (Carpentry Stories "the novel" Kanuny), B. A. Mozhayev ("Men and Women"). The content of most of the works did not leave anyone indifferent, because they dealt with human problems. Writers and villagers not only recorded deep changes in consciousness, the morality of the village man, but also showed a more dramatic side of these shifts, affecting the changes in the connection of generations, the transmission of the spiritual experience of the older generations younger.

Violation of the continuity of traditions led to the extinction of the old Russian villages with their centuries of life, language, morality. Replaced comes a new way of rural life, close to urban. As a result, the fundamental concept of village life is changing - the concept of "home", in which since ancient times Russian people have also invested the concept of "fatherland", "native land". Through the understanding of this concept was carried out and a deep connection between generations.

Yu. V. Trifonov, who was interested in the moral problems of his contemporaries (the stories "The Exchange", "Another Life", "The Old Man"), became the recognized leader of "everyday" prose. The same genre includes the novels of Y. Bondarev "The Shore" and "Choice", the novel by B. Vasilyev "The Last Day" and "Do not Shoot the White Swans."

A special place in art was taken by books and films by V. M. Shukshin, who displayed images of "strange" people from the people and reflected a turning point in their minds under the influence of the onset of urban culture on rural ones.

The author of the popular moral-conflict moral plays "The Eldest Son", "Duck Hunt", and "Last Summer in Chulimsk" was playwright A. V. Vampilov.

The work of national writers was very popular in the country and abroad: Kirghiz Aitmatov (the novels "Jamil", "Farewell to Gulsary", "The White Ship", "And the Day Lasts for More Than a Century", etc.), the Belarusian V. Bykov ("It does not hurt the dead", "Kruglyansky bridge", "Sotnikov", etc.), Georgian N. Dumbadze (the story "I, grandmother, Iliko and Hilarion", "I see the sun", the novel "White flags"), Estonian Ian Cross (novels "Between the Three Fads", "The Imperial Madman").

In the 1960s, the work of the Russian poet N. Rubtsov, who had died early (1971), falls on the market. Extremely simple stylistics, melodious intonation, sincerity, and unbreakable connection with the Motherland are peculiar to his lyrics.

The composer G. V. Sviridov devoted his musical works to the theme of the motherland, its fate ("Kursk Songs", "Pushkin's Wreath", suites "Time, Forward", musical illustration of A. S. Pushkin's story "The Snowstorm").

The 1970s were a time for the rise of Soviet theatrical art. The Moscow Drama and Comedy Theater on Taganka was especially popular with the advanced public. On his stage were "The Good Man of Sesuana" by B. Brecht, "Ten Days That Shook the World" by J. Reed, "And the Dawns Here are Quiet ..." B. Vasiliev, "House on the Embankment" by Y. Trifonov, "Master and Margarita" M. Bulgakov. Among other groups stood out the Leninsky Komsomol Theater, the Sovremennik Theater, the Theater named after E. Vakhtangov.

The center of the musical life remained the Academic Bolshoi Theater in Moscow. He was glorified by the names of ballet dancers G. Ulanova, M. Plisetskaya, E. Maximova, choreographers Yu. Grigorovich, V. Vasilyev, singers G. Vishnevskaya, T. Sinyavskaya, B. Rudenko, I. Arkhipova, E. Obraztsova, singers Zurab Sotkilava, V. Atlantov, E. Nesterenko.

For the whole world the name of D.F. Oistrakh, one of the leading violinists of our time, the creator of the Soviet violin school, thundered. The performing arts of pianists S. T. Richter and E. G. Gilels, violinist L. Kogan

In the 1970s, the so-called "tape revolution" began. The songs of famous bards were recorded at home and passed from hand to hand. Along with the writings of V. Vysotsky, B. Okudzhava and A. Galich, the works of Y. Vizbor, Y. Kim, A. Gorodnitsky, A. Dolsky, S. Nikitin, N. Matveyeva, E. Bachurin, V. Dolina were very popular. Everywhere there were youth clubs amateur songs, they began to be held all-Union rallies. The sympathies of youth increasingly conquered pop vocal and instrumental ensembles (VIA).

During these years, it received its own special artistic sound and one of the acute global problems of the 20th century - the problem of the relationship between man and nature. The failure to solve the problems associated with the irrational use of natural resources has also affected the human spiritual world, generated a consumer attitude to nature, heartlessness, and lack of spirituality.

In general, artistic culture has managed to set a number of pressing problems for Soviet society and tried to solve these problems in its works.

Mass and official culture. In the 1970s, two layers in artistic culture emerged - official and unofficial, that is, supported and encouraged by the state and not recognized by it. Both he and other layers included both highly artistic samples and weak works. In samizdat went not only works of Brodsky and Nabokov, but low-grade detectives. Conversely, the official culture was not exhausted only by works with a pronounced ideological orientation.

The narrow framework of officially allowed ideas, themes and forms could not accommodate the whole variety of creative possibilities. Freedom of society from the fear that engulfed society during the personality cult, and the emergence of technical distribution opportunities led to the expansion of informal culture. The "kitchen" disputes of the Moscow intelligentsia, as well as the resumption of disputes between Westernizers and Slavophiles, became a peculiar phenomenon of the informal culture.

RUSSIAN NATIONAL CULTURE AND "RESTRUCTURING" («PERESTROIKA»)

The renewal of the system of state socialism begun by the party leadership headed by M. S. Gorbachev in 1985 had great consequences for all branches of culture. In the course of "perestroika" (1985-1991), an intensive break-up of stereotypes in all directions of social and cultural life developed. For six years, the situation in cultural life has changed radically. The monolith of "Soviet culture", artificially fastened by ideological dogmas, disappeared. Cultural life has become incomparably more complex, diverse, multivariate.

Perestroika as a process of transformation of Soviet society is closely connected with culture, which played a huge role in the spiritual preparation of change. Culture has become the core of the ideological reconfiguration of society.

The policy of publicity was crucial for changes in the cultural life of the society. Reformers viewed glasnost as a necessary condition for democratization and the acceleration of socio-economic development. The postulates of the official ideology were softened or partially revised. The class approach, with its ideological irreconcilability, was gradually crowded out by the idea of the priority of universal human values and "socialist pluralism" of opinions. However, the pluralism of opinions allowed from above very quickly went beyond the socialist framework.

For "perestroika", ideological differences and political delimitation of the artistic intelligentsia are characteristic, which once divided creative unions. From the ceremonial official events, congresses of the creative intelligentsia turned into discussions. New groups appeared, although their organizational design was constrained by the difficulty of sharing property owned by the unions.

The instability of the political and economic situation and the easing of the exit procedure led to a new wave of emigration from the country. The normalization of relations with the Russian Diaspora and modern means of transport and communication helped to maintain the unity of Russian culture. In the USSR, the emigrant periodical began to be sold freely.

The weakening of censorship caused a stormy stream of publications on previously forbidden topics. The discussion and condemnation of the "deformations of socialism", which had accumulated quite a lot in the 70 years of Soviet power, came to the fore. Sixties prevailed among the authors of sharply critical journalistic articles.

The 1980s - the time of concentration of artistic culture around the idea of repentance. The motive of universal sin, plachha forces to resort to such forms of artistic figurative thinking as a parable, a myth, a symbol (T. Abuladze's film "Repentance" by C. Aitmatov, the film "Repentance").

Mitigation of ideological dictates allowed us to expand the cultural and informational space in which society lived. The mass reader gained access to literature, which for decades hid in spetskhranah. For two or three years, "fat" literary and art magazines returned to the readers dozens of works by previously banned authors. The border between censored literature and samizdat blurred. On the screens came back "bookshelf" (not missed by the censorship at the time) films, to the scenes of theaters - "old new" plays. The rehabilitation of dissidents began. A characteristic phenomenon of the spiritual life of the late 1980s was the rethinking of the history of the Soviet period. Once again, there was a peculiar confirmation of the idea that not only the future is unpredictable in Russia, but also the past. Began to publish documents that were previously inaccessible even to specialists. There was a surge of interest in nonfiction and documentary prose. The most important feature of the artistic situation of the eighties - is the emergence of a powerful stream of "returned" artistic culture. The Russian public had the opportunity to discover for themselves the names and works, which were widely known in the West, that were previously deliberately banished from Russian culture: Nobel Prize Winners B. L. Pasternak, A. I. Solzhenitsyn, I. Brodsky, and V. V. Nabokov, E. Limonov, V. Aksenov, M. Shemyakin, Ernst Neizvestnyj, etc.

CONCLUSION

The main characteristics of Soviet culture in this period were:

- 1950-1960s.: "OTTEPEL" in the cultural life of the society - weakening of censorship, democratization of relations between government and culture.
- 1953: Establishment of the USSR Ministry of Culture.
- Appeal to Western cultural patterns - international cultural exchange
- Rehabilitation of a number of cultural and scientific figures repressed during the Stalinist regime: S. S. Prokofiev, D. D. Shostakovich, A. D. Sakharov.
- After 1964: Tightening control over the cultural life of society (banning criticism of the personality cult, stopping the de-Stalinization process).

- Tight control over the activities of the intelligentsia.
- Increased ideological pressure on cultural figures.
- 1966 – 1988: Mass emigration of a number of cultural figures (some were expelled, many decided to leave the country on their own): E. Unknown, I. Brodsky, A. Solzhenitsyn, V. Aksenov and others.
- The birth of a bard song.

In terms of the diversity of creative styles, aesthetic concepts, and attachments to a particular artistic tradition, the culture of the late 1980s and early 1990s resembles the beginning of the 20th century in Russian culture.

Domestic culture seems to get the failed natural moment of its development (quietly passed by the Western European culture of the 20th century) and forcibly stopped by well-known social and political events in our country. At the same time, the elimination of censorship and the policy of "open doors" in cultural exchange also had a negative side. Hundreds of preachers of various denominations, religious schools and sects, which formed their branches in the USSR, rushed into the country. In place of ideological dictates in art came the dictates of the market. The stream of mass Western culture poured low-quality domestic products. By the end of Perestroika, the state cultural policy had to solve fundamentally new tasks: how to ensure the support of a high level of national culture in market conditions and civilized measures to regulate the spread of mass culture.

REFERENCES

Aristarkhov, V. V., & Anisimov, E. A. (2015). *Basics of the state cultural policy*. Moscow, Russia: Ministry of Culture of the Russian Federation. Retrieved from http://www.folkcentr.ru/wp-content/uploads/2017/03/Basic-GKP.pdf

Komissarov, S. S. (2011). Politics in the sphere of culture: the vector of spiritual revival of the national civilization. *Bulletin of Moscow State University of Culture and Art, 1*. Retrieved from https://cyberleninka.ru/article/n/politika-v-sfere-kultury-vektor-duhovnogo-vozrozhdeniya-otechestvennoy-tsivilizatsii

Leksin, V. N. (2015). The Great Culture of the Great War. *Outlines of Global Transformations: Politics, Economics, Law, 3*(41). Retrieved from https://cyberleninka.ru/article/n/velikaya-kultura-velikoy-voyny. (in Russian)

Plaggenborg, S. (2000). Revolution and culture. In *Cultural landmarks in the period between the October Revolution and the era of Stalinism* (pp. 287-321). Saint Petersburg, Russia: Academic Press.

Rolf, M. (2009). *Soviet mass holidays. Moscow, Russia*: ROSSPEN.

Ryabenko, V. (2014). *Soviet culture in the years of the Great Patriotic War and in the post-war period.* Retrieved from https://magref.ru/sovetskaya-kultura-v-godyi-velikoy-otechestvennoy-voynyi-i-v-poslevoennyiy-period (in Russian)

Sazhina, A. I. (2015). The state policy of the Soviet government in the field of education and enlightenment of the adult population in 1917-1927. Astrakhan, Russia: Academic Press.

Stradina, E. A. (2007). State policy of Russia in the field of culture in the context of the reform of the political system. Yaroslavl, Russia: Academic Press.

Suanova, R. E. (2012). State policy in the field of culture in 1917-1941. (on materials of North Ossetia). Vladikavkaz, Russia: Academic Press.

Sviridov, E. G. (2014). State policy of the USSR in the sphere of festive culture (20s-40s). *The Times of Science, 2.* Retrieved from https://cyberleninka.ru/article/n/gosudarstvennaya-politika-sssr-v-sfere-prazdnichnoy-kultury-20-40-e-gg

The project. (2014, May 16). *Fundamentals of the state cultural policy.* Retrieved from https://rg.ru/2014/05/15/osnovi-dok.html

Yeleskina, O. V. (2005). State policy in the field of culture. Kemerovo, Russia: Academic Press.

Zakovich, N. M., Kosuha, P. I., & Perunov, V. A. (1986). Socialist rites. Kiev, Ukraine: Academic Press.

Zakovich, N. M., & Zots, V. A. (1980). Holidays and rituals as an element of Soviet culture. *Questions of Scientific Atheism,* (26), 165-177.

Chapter 8
New Trends in Cultural Life in the Post-Soviet Period

Igor Asmarov
Voronezh State Institute of Arts, Russia

ABSTRACT

Modern Russian culture is very different from Soviet culture, but they have many similarities, too. In essence, this is the same country, only without national margins and the former allied national republics. But within the country, multinationality remains since Russia is a federal state with many peoples of diverse cultures. Russian culture is the culture of a multinational country. Modern Russian culture has lost the features of ideological and party (communist) dependence, but retains the influence of the state, like any other culture of any country in the world. True, the influence of the state on the culture in each country goes to a greater or lesser extent. In Russia, this state influence on culture is very large up to the present day, and it has a pronounced dualistic character. On one hand, Russian culture is provided with financial assistance "from above", and on the other hand, some kind of framework is created that cannot be crossed, almost as it was in Soviet times, when the state order in the cultural sphere dominated.

DOI: 10.4018/978-1-5225-9985-2.ch008

INTRODUCTION

New trends in cultural life in the post-Soviet period in Russia have emerged thanks to the elimination of the former Marxist-Leninist communist ideology. Nevertheless, the impact of the political situation on culture and art remained and are important dominant factors in the work of writers, artists, sculptors, etc.

Since by the mid-1980s the Soviet state had exhausted most of its creative forces, it came to the stage of stagnation and reappraisal of socialist ideals due to their sharp divergence from the realities of life, the new Communist Party leader M. S. Gorbachev announced a course on the so-called "restructuring". In the period of perestroika, which began with a new cultural policy, advocating publicity and pluralism of opinions, there was a "return" of the creative heritage of artists who had previously been ideologically banned (A. I. Solzhenitsyn, B. L. Pasternak, M. A. Bulgakov, V. V. Nabokov and others.). However, the educational system and fundamental science, which have been the subject of national pride for a long time, as a result of unsuccessful reforming, come to a state of crisis, from which they have not yet emerged. The lack of state support, the decline of prestige and the loss of understanding of the social importance of the scientist's work led to a brain drain abroad, leaving them in commerce and other areas of activity.

In the post-Soviet period,. which began with the collapse of the USSR (1991), the "shock" reforms and the radical reorganization of society and the state on the paths to the establishment of liberal democracy, many social norms and values of the socialist past, including deeply positive ones, were lost: respect for work, the rejection of exploitativeness and the desire for profit, the spirit of collectivism and mutual assistance, social justice. Russian culture again experienced revolutionary changes in the root. The state has freed itself from the role of censor in culture, ideological control has disappeared and the centralized cultural policy has gone into the past. At the same time, the single spiritual and ideological core of culture disappeared, which created freedom both for cultural creation and moral and spiritual degradation. The transitional character of the post-Soviet period in the culture of Russia is quite obvious, the future results of which are difficult to predict. However, among the main trends shaping the shape of a new culture, the following should be highlighted.

The transition to market relations led to the emergence of mass culture, expressed in show business, commercial forms of pop, music and cinematographic art, which in general significantly reduced the level of artistic creativity.

Postmodern tendencies perceived from Western culture are also characters for modern Russia. Postmodern propagandizes pluralism, rejection of all canons, norms and traditions, absolute truths, and recognizes as equivalent any cultural phenomena to which countries and historical epochs they belong to. The desire for eclecticism, the connection of the incompatible, daring experimentation in recent decades has manifested itself in Russian culture, which can be assessed ambivalent. For example, in literary works, new reference points gave rise to such undoubtedly talented writers as V. O. Pelevin (the novel "Chapaev and the Void", etc.). However, taken seriously and brought to its logical conclusion postmodern with its skeptical attitude to absolute values can erode the national foundations of cultural life, detrimental effect on the morals and spiritual health of modern generations.

The atmosphere of spiritual vacuum, which arose in Soviet times and was most acutely felt at the time of the collapse of the entire social and cultural system, caused a burning spiritual thirst for a large part of Russian society of the post-reform period. She poured into various forms. On the one hand, with the fall of the Iron Curtain, Russia's cultural space began to rapidly fill with new religious teachings and sects (Eastern cults, occultism, neo-shamanism, neo-paganism, missionary activity of American Protestants). On the other hand, the revival of traditional religiosity and the Orthodox foundations of Russian culture began, expressed in the mass conversion of former Soviet atheists. In the cinema of Russia of the first decade of the 21st century, the P. S. Lungin "Island" (2006), which received many national awards. It is noteworthy that the main character of the film, the holy father of Anatoly, was played by P. N. Mamonov. The rock musician and the founder of the Zvuki Mu group experienced a real spiritual rebirth in the post-Soviet era, along with many other key figures of the Russian rock generation of the 1980s, such as Yu. Yu. Shevchuk (leader of the musical group "DDT"), and K. E. Kinchev (leader of the musical group "Alice").

The beginning of the 1990s was marked by the accelerated disintegration of the single culture of the USSR into separate national cultures, which not only rejected the values of the common culture of the USSR, but also the cultural traditions of each other. Such a sharp opposition of various national cultures led to an increase in socio-cultural tensions, to the emergence of military conflicts and later caused the disintegration of a single socio-cultural space.

But the processes of cultural development are not interrupted with the collapse of state structures and the fall of political regimes. The culture of new Russia is organically connected with all previous periods of the country's history. At the same time, the new political and economic situation could not but affect the culture.

Its relations with the authorities have radically changed. The state has ceased to dictate its demands to culture, and the culture has lost its guaranteed customer.

The common core of cultural life has disappeared - a centralized system of governance and a unified cultural policy. Determining ways of further cultural development has become the business of the society itself and the subject of sharp disagreements. The search range is extremely wide - from following Western patterns to the apology of isolationism. The absence of a unifying sociocultural idea is perceived by a part of society as a manifestation of a deep crisis in which Russian culture found itself by the end of the 20th century. Others consider cultural pluralism to be the natural norm of a civilized society.

The elimination of ideological barriers created favorable opportunities for the development of spiritual culture. However, the economic crisis experienced by the country, the difficult transition to market relations increased the danger of commercialization of culture, the loss of national traits in the course of its further development, the negative impact of the Americanization of certain spheres of culture (primarily musical life and cinema) as a kind of retribution for "introducing universal values ".

The spiritual sphere is experiencing a sharp crisis in the middle of 1990s. In a difficult transition period, the role of spiritual culture as a treasury of moral guidelines for society increases, politicization of culture and cultural figures leads to the implementation of its unusual functions for it, and deepens the polarization of society. The desire to direct countries to the rails of market development leads to the impossibility of the existence of certain spheres of culture that objectively need state support. The possibility of the so-called "free" development of culture on the basis of the low cultural needs of fairly wide strata of the population leads to an increase in spiritlessness, the promotion of violence and, as a result, an increase in crime.

At the same time, the division between elite and mass forms of culture, between the youth environment and the older generation, continues to deepen. All these processes unfold against the background of a rapid and sharp increase in uneven access to consumption, not only material but cultural goods.

In the sociocultural situation that developed in Russian society by the mid-1990s, man, as a living system representing the unity of the physical and spiritual, natural and socio-cultural, hereditary and acquired in vivo, can no longer develop normally. Indeed, as people strengthen their market relations, most people are increasingly alienated from the values of national culture. And this is a completely logical trend for the type of society that is being created in Russia at the end of the 20th century. All this, which has become a reality over the past decade, brings society to the limit of accumulation of explosive social energy.

The modern period of development of national culture can be described as transitional. For the second time in a century, a real cultural revolution took place in Russia. In modern Russian culture manifest numerous and very contradictory trends. But they can, relatively speaking, be combined into two groups.

First: destructive and crisis tendencies, which contribute to the complete subordination of Russian culture to the standards of Western civilization.

The second: progressive trends, fueled by the ideas of patriotism, collectivism, social justice, traditionally understood and professed by the peoples of Russia.

The struggle between these essentially antagonistic tendencies will probably determine the main direction of development of the national culture of the third millennium.

Russian culture and the era of “postmodern”. Modern cultural processes taking place in Russia are an inseparable part of the global development of the end of the 20th - beginning of the 21st centuries, the transition from industrial to post-industrial society, from “modern” to “postmodern”.

The spiritual state of Western culture and art of modernity is called postmodernism. It was born from the tragic realization of the impossibility of restoring universal harmony through the exaltation of the individual. The main value of postmodernism is “radical multiplicity.” According to the German researcher of the problems of modern culture V. Welsh, this multiplicity is not a synthesis, but an eclectic combination of heterogeneous elements, blurring the boundaries between the creator of values and their consumer, between the center and the periphery, turning values into antisymbols by losing their deep connections with the spiritual component of culture.

Thus, in the world of postmodernism, there is a dehierarchization of culture, making it impossible to establish a new value system. By virtue of this, modern man is doomed to remain in a state of spiritual amorphism. He is able to observe everything, but nothing can draw it from the inside. Therefore, external forms of restriction of people who in every way seek to strengthen the Western world through fashion, public opinion, standardization of life, increasing its comfort, etc., become so necessary.

For the same reasons, mass media began to occupy the first place in culture. They were even given the name of the "fourth force", meaning the other three - legislative, executive and judicial.

In modern Russian culture, incompatible values and orientations are wonderfully combined: collectivism, conciliarism and individualism, egoism, deliberate politicization and demonstrative apoliticality, statehood and anarchy, and so on. Indeed, today, as if on equal, such non-coexisting but each other are mutually exclusive phenomena, such as the newly acquired cultural values of the Russian emigre, the newly rethought classical heritage, the values of official Soviet culture.

Thus, the general picture of the cultural life of Russia is typical for postmodernism, which was widespread in the world by the end of our century. This is a special type of world view, aimed at the rejection of all norms and traditions, the establishment of any truths, focused on unrestrained pluralism, recognition of any cultural manifestations as equivalent. But postmodernism is not able to reconcile the irreconcilable, since it does not put forward fruitful ideas for this, it only combines contrasts as the source material for further cultural and historical creativity.

In difficult historical and natural conditions, Russia has survived, has created its own original culture, fertilized by the influence of both the West and the East, and, in turn, has enriched other cultures with its influence. Modern domestic culture faces a difficult task - to develop its strategic course for the future in a rapidly changing world. The solution of this global task is extremely difficult, as it rests on the need to understand the deep-seated contradictions inherent in our culture throughout its entire historical development.

Russian culture may well provide an answer to the challenges of the modern world. But for this, it is necessary to move on to such forms of its self-awareness, which would cease to reproduce the same mechanisms of irreconcilable struggle, tough confrontation, the absence of a "middle". It is imperative to get away from thinking, focusing on maximalism, a radical coup and reorganization of the world as soon as possible.

MODERN MODELS OF DEVELOPMENT OF MULTINATIONAL CULTURE OF RUSSIA

The time of troubles, which our culture is experiencing now, is not a new phenomenon, but constantly recurring, and the culture has always found certain answers to the challenges of the time, continued to evolve. The whole world was at a crossroads at the turn of the 21st century, we are talking about changing the very type of culture, which was formed within the framework of Western civilization over the past few centuries.

The revival of culture is the most important condition for the renewal of our society. Determining ways of further cultural development has become the subject of heated debates in society, because the state has ceased to dictate its demands to culture, the centralized system of governance and a unified cultural policy have disappeared.

One of the existing points of view is that the state should not interfere in the affairs of culture, since this is fraught with the establishment of its new dictate over culture, and culture itself will find the means for its survival.

Another point of view seems to be more substantiated, the essence of which is that while ensuring freedom of culture, the right to cultural identity, the state assumes the development of strategic tasks of cultural construction and the duty to protect cultural and historical national heritage, the necessary financial support for cultural values.

The state must realize that culture cannot be left at the mercy of business, its support, including education, science, is of paramount importance for maintaining the moral and mental health of the nation. The crisis of spirituality causes strong mental discomfort in many people, since the mechanism of identification with super-personal values is seriously damaged. Without this mechanism, no culture exists, and in modern Russia all super-personal values have become dubious.

Despite all the contradictory characteristics of national culture, society cannot allow separation from its cultural heritage. Disintegrating culture is little adapted to transformations, for the impulse to creative changes comes from values that are cultural categories. Only an integrated and strong national culture can relatively easily adapt new goals to its values, master new patterns of behavior.

In this regard, in modern Russia, there are three possible models for the development of multinational culture:

- a victory of cultural and political conservatism; an attempt to stabilize the situation on the basis of ideas about Russia's originality and its special way in history. In this case:
- there is a return to the nationalization of culture,
- automatic support of cultural heritage, traditional forms of creativity,
- foreign influence on culture is limited,

- Russian art classics remain a subject of worship, and aesthetic innovations are suspicious.
- By its nature, this model is short-lived and inevitably leads to a new crisis, but in thc conditions of Russia it can exist for a long time;

Russia's integration from outside into the world economic and cultural system and its transformation into a "province" in relation to global centers. When approving this model:

- there is a "McDonalization" of the national culture,
- the cultural life of society is stabilized on the basis of commercial self-regulation.

The key challenge is the preservation of a distinctive national culture, its international influence and the integration of cultural heritage into society;

Russia's integration into the system of universal culture as an equal participant in world art processes. To implement this model, it is necessary to fully utilize the cultural potential, to fundamentally reorient state cultural policy, to ensure accelerated development of the domestic cultural industry within the country, to fully encourage the inclusion of artists in the global networks of artistic production and communication. It is this model that deserves resolute support, for it is focused on a culture that should actively influence both politics, the economy, and the spiritual life.

Thus, modern Russian culture is the most complex and ambiguous phenomenon. On the one hand, it has always defined the trends of the sociocultural process in the world, on the other hand, it has been influenced by Western culture in the broad sense of the word.

Domestic culture in the era of modern times has gone through several of the most significant stages: pre-Soviet (until 1917); the Soviet (until 1985) and the modern stage of democratic change. At all these stages, the large role of the state in the development of culture, the relative passivity of the population, the large gap between the culture of the masses and its most prominent representatives manifested itself.

Having embarked on the path of capitalist development later than the leading countries of the West, in the pre-reform years Russia managed to achieve much in the field of economics. In the spiritual respect, Russia at the turn of the 19th-20th centuries gave world culture a number of outstanding achievements. The controversial nature of the development of culture in the Soviet period led to the accumulation of numerous contradictions, the resolution of which has not yet been completed.

The orientation of the development of culture in the future will be determined by many factors, primarily the liberation from external dependence, taking into account Russia's originality and the experience of its historical development. At the turn of the millennium, Russia again found itself at a crossroads. But no matter how its fate, the Russian culture remains the main wealth of the country and the key to the unity of the nation.

At the turn of the millennium, mankind has been challenged in the form of global problems, in the face of which it will act as a single entity that makes conscious and coordinated decisions. In this creation of universal unity, the decisive role belongs to the mutually enriching dialogue of different cultures, the world cultural process.

Russian culture has long played an important role in this process. Russia has a special civilizing and organizing function in the world socio-cultural space. Russian culture has proved its viability, has confirmed that the development of democracy, moral purification is impossible without the preservation and enhancement of the accumulated cultural potential. Russia is a country of great literature and art, a bold science and a recognized educational system, ideal aspirations for universal human values, cannot but be one of the most active creators of the culture of the world.

In the 20th century, Russian culture has experienced a radical breakdown of the traditions of the old, monarchical Russia, the construction of a fundamentally new type of culture based on the values of socialism. The collapse of the Soviet state at the end of the century led to another sharp change of values. In the catastrophic 1990s for the country, the main ways of further development were outlined, among which there are health-improving trends towards the revival of the spiritual core of the primordial Russian culture, as well as trends related to the costs of a market society in the form of mass culture based on hedonism and consumption orientation. It is not easy to predict the future shape of a native culture, but it is clear that it will depend on the ability of a modern person to recognize true values.

THE MAIN TRENDS IN THE DEVELOPMENT OF RUSSIAN CULTURE AT THE END OF THE XXTH CENTURY

Russian culture is in search of new spiritual and moral ideals. Since the mid-1980s Communist ideology, which formerly formed the basis of the worldview of the majority of society, has entered a period of serious crisis. Official ideologues could not explain the processes and phenomena occurring in their country and in the world. Against the background of the collapse of the world socialist system, and then the USSR, the communist idea ceased to be popular. People tried to realize their place in the world with the help of other ideological, religious and philosophical concepts. The "revolution from above", which began in Russia in 1991, was accompanied not only by the refusal of communist ideas, but also by many traditional, centuries-old values, customs and traditions. The widespread use of foreign economic and political models inevitably led to the adoption of Western (mostly liberal) spiritual values based not on traditional collectivism, but on individualism, on the priority of not spiritual, but the material principle.

Changed and public expectations. If, prior to perestroika, a significant part of the population still believed in official propaganda and the idea of building communism in the final perspective, then from the beginning of the 90s. this belief was replaced by the expectation of building the "people's capitalism" promised in a short time by the authorities. As economic policy failures and problems in interethnic relations grew, public sentiment began to change again. Liberal ideas were perceived by a significant part of society as alien. Gradually, interest in national culture, traditional spiritual values, old films, songs, and folk traditions returned. On this basis, the ideas of nationalism became especially popular for a part of the population. True, social consciousness has not returned to the path of support even for a renewed communist ideology. It turned out to be ready to accept a rather national-liberal ideological concept. One of the main features of the spiritual life of society in the 90s. there was a real ideological pluralism: all prohibitions and restrictions on any ideological teachings (except those that called for violence, social and national hostility) were removed by law.

THE INFLUENCE OF RELIGION AND THE CHURCH ON THE PUBLIC CONSCIOUSNESS

The crisis of social ideals and the prevailing value system has always been accompanied by the conversion of people to faith. Also the crisis of communist ideology at the turn of the 1980s-90s. caused a rapid surge of religious sentiment in society. By the mid-1990s, according to opinion polls, up to 34% of the country's adult population considered themselves believers, and another 35% fluctuated between faith and disbelief. Across the country, restoration and construction of temples, mosques, synagogues, and datsans took place. In Moscow, in just 5 years, the Cathedral of Christ the Savior was restored, built in the 19th century. with the money of millions of ordinary people in memory of the great victory in the Patriotic War of 1812. Now it has become a symbol of Russia's spiritual rebirth. Religious literature, published in large print runs, has become in great demand. However, the collapse of the Soviet Union entailed heavy consequences for the Orthodox Church.

In the Baltics, the authorities demanded the transfer of parishes and property of the Russian Orthodox Church under the control of the Constantinople Patriarchate. In Ukraine, a small group of church leaders announced the autocephaly (independence) of the Ukrainian Orthodox Church. This caused a split of Orthodoxy in Ukraine, which, moreover, is experiencing aggressive pressure from the Uniate Church. With the support of the authorities, the Uniates by force seized almost all Orthodox churches in the western regions of Ukraine. Mass pilgrimages of Orthodox Christians to Jerusalem and Muslims to Mecca were resumed. However, the democratization of political and spiritual life, on the one hand, and the religious illiteracy of yesterday's atheists, on the other, led to the expansion of various religious sects and movements, including radical ones, into Russia. For the first time, traditional religious denominations had to take care of maintaining their positions in the struggle for the minds of believers.

LITERATURE AND ART

On the development of national culture in the 1990s. Three major external factors had a significant impact: the removal of restrictions on the freedom of creativity; a sharp reduction in government allocations for the development of cultural institutions; a serious decline in the general cultural level of the population. "The law of the pendulum" led to the fact that the method of socialist realism was quickly forgotten in the late 80s. Many cultural figures rushed to the approval of unusual and seemingly tempting conceptualism, postmodernism, neo-avant-gardism, and other artistic trends. However, this led to the "elitization" of art, which was interesting in most of its narrow circle of specialists and admirers. Those works of literature and art, which in the 90s. gained international recognition, were created in the traditional, realistic manner. For example, in 1995, the Academy Award "Oscar" was awarded the film "Burnt by the Sun" by N. Mikhalkov, and in 1996 the S. Prisoner's Captive film by S. Bodrov was awarded with a special prize from the Cannes Film Festival. The growing interest in the history and traditions of the people is reflected in another film by N. Mikhalkov - "The Siberian Barber" (1999). New, unusual phenomena of life, characteristic of the 90s, were embodied in the films of V. Todorovsky "Country of the Deaf", A. Balabanov "Brother" and "Brother-2", A. Khotinenko "Muslim" and others. The tradition was revived Moscow International Film Festivals. The All-Russian Kinotavr Film Festival in Sochi was held annually. However, the number of films produced by film studios in the country has noticeably decreased. New phenomena have occurred in the Russian literature. The creative crisis marked the mastery of those writers who in past years acted as apologists for the Soviet system. For most Soviet-era writers, the creation of non-fiction pieces was characteristic, most of which criticized the character that began in the 1990s. social transformation. This was mentioned, in particular, in the collection of articles by the famous dissident V. Maksimov "Self-Destruction", journalistic articles by A. Solzhenitsyn, L. Borodin, V. Belov, poetry-reflections of S. Vikulov "My People" (1993), etc. The writers experienced in the 90s. and the identity crisis in the conditions of disintegration of a single state (the story of F. Iskander "Pshad", etc.). New circumstances of life and its heroes ("new Russians", unemployed, refugees, homeless, etc.) are reflected in the story 3. Boguslavskaya "Facing South: Sketch for the portrait of "new Russians". Nostalgic sadness for the outgoing lifestyle, longing for the ideal of purity and purity of patriarchal Russia sounded in the works of V. Rasputin. It is characteristic that in the 90s. He became one of the pioneers of the new trend in Russian literature - "post-village prose." The focus of his new works ("In one Siberian city", "Young Russia", etc.) turned out to be the problems of city life, the ideals of the urban intelligentsia. The fruit of L. Leonov's many years of spiritual evolution was his last novel, The Pyramid (1994), in which the author speaks about the contradictions of progress, his attitude towards Orthodoxy and the church. In his novel "Cursed and Murdered" V. Astafyev summed up his many years of meditation on heroism, degerization and pacifism, showed the war from the most unattractive side, emphasizing the unbearable conditions of military labor and life. In the book of V. Aksyonov, "The New Sweet Style" (1998), the writer's attitude to the external and internal state of modern man is expressed.

The 1990s are characterized by the emergence of many new names in Russian literature. One of the most popular young writers was Viktor Pelevin, known for his two novels "Chapaev and Emptiness" and "Generation P", which feature not only fantastic plots, but also a philosophical, metaphysical, ironic and grotesque attitude to everything Soviet. A fresh look at the world around us and an unusual combination of modern themes and genre-style legends distinguished the work of Yuri Buida ("People on the Island", "Don Domino").

As part of the postmodern approaches, Dmitri Prigov (his collection "Fifty drops of blood") created his poems. Prize them. Apollo Grigoriev in 2000 was awarded the book of poems by the poet-avant-garde artist Viktor Sosnora "Where did you go? And where is the window?" Recognized leaders of metaphoric poetry of the 90s. became Alexander Eremenko ("The huge volume was flipped at random ...") and Ivan Zhdanov ("The Prophet"). The main feature of the new literary works was the irony over the Soviet past and the search for unusual forms of self-expression of the authors. The transition to market relations put representatives of the creative intelligentsia in unusual conditions for them: on the one hand, the state for the first time lifted all bans on creativity, but on the other, it practically stopped the former financing of creative activity. "Discovery of the West" turned out to be not only an acquaintance with the best sides of its culture, but also a flood of low-grade fakes that had poured into the country. This could not but lead to the erosion of many features of the traditional morality of Russians, the decline of morals, the growth of crime (Zamaraev, 2016).

Thus, the development of national science and culture in the 1990s wore the same contradictory character as in other areas of life: on the one hand, the creative intelligentsia gained complete freedom of expression, but on the other, deprived of financial support from the state in the market conditions and a sharp drop in the desire of the majority of the population to become familiar with cultural values able to realize their full potential (Zezina, 1990).

We will also say a few more words about cinematography in Russia in the 1990s. The economic crisis, political instability and general confusion had an impact on post-Soviet cinema. The main impression of the films of that era - some hopeless darkness and despair. Apparently, this is typical for any transitional and crisis periods. In the Russian cinema, the tendency to "blacken" the entire Soviet past has not yet disappeared. In addition, in all areas of culture, until recently, actively copied Western samples. Unfortunately, the fall of the USSR opened up access to all that heresy and vulgarity, which barely leaked through the iron curtain. Sexual revolution, vulgarity were raised to a cult. The mistakes of that period we are reaping so far. Culture was and remains the most sensitive component of society, therefore, gave out all sorts of nonsense under the brand of "quality".

This period is not just a difficult milestone, this is what Russia needed to go through after such difficult events as the collapse of the USSR and complete chaos in politics. Culture was divided into two camps: a real culture, something of which represents and brings people benefit, and creations without meaning and without soul, that is, complete creative nonsense. People sought to use all this vulgarity and nonsense, so the generation of empty-headed citizens has grown. But the true Russian culture still existed and tried not to suffocate in this stench. If someone positively perceives collectivism and is drawn to the spiritual, then he is on his way to a monastery. The fact of the matter is that a person thinks, first of all, about himself, a person is mercantile, and there is no need to deal with this, as in the years of military communism. Individualism is a normal phenomenon in the life of society and in the sphere of culture, and it is not all from the West that has come, but has lived within ourselves for centuries, since we are all ordinary people.

CONCLUSION

The most characteristic features of Russian culture and Russian art at the end of the 20th and in the beginning of the 21st centuries were commercialization, the absence of ideological restrictions, the enormous influence of Western popular culture, and the enormous influence of the state on the cultural life of the country. This is due to the fact that the state provides funding for culture in many areas, in the field of cinema, theater, painting and music, etc.

Therefore, many cultural projects in Russia come not only from the private sector (although such projects are taking place), but precisely from the public sector and funding received from the Government of Russia through the Ministry of Culture of the Russian Federation and regional Departments of Culture, which give money for various cultural programs of the country.

REFERENCES

Ashmarov, I. A. (2004). Institutional space of Belarus, Russia, Ukraine. Political, socio-economic and cultural aspects of cooperation between Russia and Ukraine: history and modernity: materials between. In *Scientific and practical conf.* Voronezh, Russia: Voronezh State University. (in Russian)

Ashmarov, I. A., & Karpyuk, D. A. (2008). Problems of globalization of modern civilization. In Problems of modern humanism in the "risk society": Proceedings of a regional scientific conference. Voronezh, Russia: Voronezh State Technical University. (in Russian)

Ashmarov, I. A., & Latysheva, L. P. (2008). Culture and Civilization: Contradiction or Unity? In The clash of civilizations and the dialogue of cultures: the challenges and answers of modernity: the proceedings of a regional scientific conference. Voronezh, Russia: Voronezh State Technical University. (in Russian)

Balakina, T. I. (2000). *World Art. Russia 9th - beg. 20th century.* Moscow, Russia: Academic Press. (in Russian)

Belova, T. (1991). *Culture and power.* Moscow, Russia: Academic Press. (in Russian)

Culture of the post-war decade - Russia. (n.d.). Retrieved from http://russia.rin.ru/guides/7170.html (in Russian)

Culture: theories and problems. (1995). Moscow, Russia: Academic Press. (in Russian)

Dorogova, L. N. (n.d.). Soviet Culture and Modern Russia. *Culturology.* Retrieved from http://web-local.rudn.ru/web-local/uem/ido/1/cult/cu3-7.html (in Russian)

Dorogova, L. N., Pykhanov, Yu. V., & Mareeva, E. V. (n.d.). *Culturology: Electronic textbook.* Retrieved from http://ido.rudn.ru/ffec/cult-index.html (in Russian)

Dracha, G. V. (Ed.). (2000). *Culturology.* Rostov-on-Don, Russia: Academic Press. (in Russian)

Ilina, T. V. (1994). Art History. In *Russian art.* Moscow, Russia: Academic Press. (in Russian)

Ioann (Snychev). (2001). Met. Russian symphony. St. Petersburg, Russia: Academic Press. (in Russian)

Kiselev, G. S. (1992). *The tragedy of society and man. An attempt to understand the experience of Soviet history.* Moscow, Russia: Academic Press. (in Russian)

Kondakov, I. V. (1997). *Introduction to the history of Russian culture.* Moscow, Russia: Academic Press. (in Russian)

Kravchenko, A. I. (2005). Culturology. Moscow, Russia: Academic Press. (in Russian)

Moiseev, V. V. (2010). Russian history (2nd ed.). Moscow, Russia: Moscow Institute of Economics, Management and Law. (in Russian)

Rapatskaya, L. A. (2002). Russian Art Culture: Study Guide. Moscow, Russia: Academic Press. (in Russian)

Ryabenko, V. (2014). *Soviet culture in the years of the Great Patriotic War and in the post-war period.* Retrieved from https://magref.ru/sovetskaya-kultura-v-godyi-velikoy-otechestvennoy-voynyi-i-v-poslevoennyiy-period (in Russian)

ADDITIONAL READING

Sidorov, E. Y. (1998). Culture of Peace and Culture of Russia. *Polis (Bologna)*, *C*(5), 106–113. (in Russian)

Related Readings

To continue IGI Global's long-standing tradition of advancing innovation through emerging research, please find below a compiled list of recommended IGI Global book chapters and journal articles in the areas of Russia, economics, and politics. These related readings will provide additional information and guidance to further enrich your knowledge and assist you with your own research.

Abdelbary, I., & Benhin, J. K. (2019). Governance and Economic Growth in the Arab Region. In P. Zgheib (Ed.), *Impacts of Political Instability on Economics in the MENA Region* (pp. 103–133). Hershey, PA: IGI Global. doi:10.4018/978-1-5225-8247-2.ch004

Abdelbary, I., & Benhin, J. K. (2019). Political Governance and Sustainable Development: The Role of Theory. In P. Zgheib (Ed.), *Impacts of Political Instability on Economics in the MENA Region* (pp. 28–73). Hershey, PA: IGI Global. doi:10.4018/978-1-5225-8247-2.ch002

Abdelbary, I., & Benhin, J. K. (2019). The Economic Reform and Political Transition: Potential and Challenges of Arab Development. In P. Zgheib (Ed.), *Impacts of Political Instability on Economics in the MENA Region* (pp. 145–184). Hershey, PA: IGI Global. doi:10.4018/978-1-5225-8247-2.ch006

Al Katheri, M. N. (2019). The Effect of the Arab Spring Revolution on the Yemeni Economy. In P. Zgheib (Ed.), *Impacts of Political Instability on Economics in the MENA Region* (pp. 134–144). Hershey, PA: IGI Global. doi:10.4018/978-1-5225-8247-2.ch005

Al Katheri, M. N., & Zgheib, P. W. (2019). Lebanese Army History and Development of Democracy: Dilemma Between Democratic Rights and National Duty. In P. Zgheib (Ed.), *Impacts of Political Instability on Economics in the MENA Region* (pp. 185–198). Hershey, PA: IGI Global. doi:10.4018/978-1-5225-8247-2.ch007

Apenko, S. N. (2018). Sustainable Project Management in the System of Economic Reform of Industries: Example of Russia. In D. Ushakov (Ed.), *Economic Reforms for Global Competitiveness* (pp. 46–62). Hershey, PA: IGI Global. doi:10.4018/978-1-5225-3856-1.ch003

Apryshchenko, V. (2019). Where Does Europe End?: European Values vs. Power Traditionalism in the Contemporary North Caucasus. In V. Apryshchenko & O. Karnaukhova (Eds.), *Memory, Identity, and Nationalism in European Regions* (pp. 98–120). Hershey, PA: IGI Global. doi:10.4018/978-1-5225-8392-9.ch005

Arkhipov, A., & Ushakov, D. (2015). Functional Effectiveness and Modern Mechanisms for National Urban Systems Globalization: The Case of Russia. In D. Ushakov (Ed.), *Urbanization and Migration as Factors Affecting Global Economic Development* (pp. 171–189). Hershey, PA: IGI Global. doi:10.4018/978-1-4666-7328-1.ch010

Ayriyan, R., & Egorov, A. (2019). The Polish Problem in the Soviet-American Relations (1944-1945): History and Memory. In V. Apryshchenko & O. Karnaukhova (Eds.), *Memory, Identity, and Nationalism in European Regions* (pp. 141–157). Hershey, PA: IGI Global. doi:10.4018/978-1-5225-8392-9.ch007

Baarda, R. (2017). Digital Democracy in Authoritarian Russia: Opportunity for Participation, or Site of Kremlin Control? In R. Luppicini & R. Baarda (Eds.), *Digital Media Integration for Participatory Democracy* (pp. 87–100). Hershey, PA: IGI Global. doi:10.4018/978-1-5225-2463-2.ch005

Bardawil, A. B., & Zgheib, P. W. (2019). The Saga of Middle East Airlines (MEA) in War and in Peace: A Case Study – A Success Story, in Spite of All Odds. In P. Zgheib (Ed.), *Impacts of Political Instability on Economics in the MENA Region* (pp. 215–242). Hershey, PA: IGI Global. doi:10.4018/978-1-5225-8247-2.ch009

Bartoszewicz, M. G. (2019). Memory as a Security Policy: The Case of Poland. In V. Apryshchenko & O. Karnaukhova (Eds.), *Memory, Identity, and Nationalism in European Regions* (pp. 50–77). Hershey, PA: IGI Global. doi:10.4018/978-1-5225-8392-9.ch003

Branch, J. (2018). A History of the Stockholm School of Economics in Riga. In O. Karnaukhova, A. Udovikina, & B. Christiansen (Eds.), *Economic and Geopolitical Perspectives of the Commonwealth of Independent States and Eurasia* (pp. 157–177). Hershey, PA: IGI Global. doi:10.4018/978-1-5225-3264-4.ch007

Breitweg, M. (2019). Collective Memory After Violent Conflict: A New Framework for Analysis. In V. Apryshchenko & O. Karnaukhova (Eds.), *Memory, Identity, and Nationalism in European Regions* (pp. 1–29). Hershey, PA: IGI Global. doi:10.4018/978-1-5225-8392-9.ch001

Campbell, A. (2016). "Imperialism" and "Federalism": The Ambiguity of State and City in Russia. In U. Sadioglu & K. Dede (Eds.), *Theoretical Foundations and Discussions on the Reformation Process in Local Governments* (pp. 353–372). Hershey, PA: IGI Global. doi:10.4018/978-1-5225-0317-0.ch015

Christiansen, B. (2018). The Effects of Globalization on the CIS and Eurasia. In O. Karnaukhova, A. Udovikina, & B. Christiansen (Eds.), *Economic and Geopolitical Perspectives of the Commonwealth of Independent States and Eurasia* (pp. 19–47). Hershey, PA: IGI Global. doi:10.4018/978-1-5225-3264-4.ch002

Dias, M. G., & Teixeira, A. A. (2018). The Importance of Geopolitical Factors in International Location Decisions: The Russian Federation Case. In O. Karnaukhova, A. Udovikina, & B. Christiansen (Eds.), *Economic and Geopolitical Perspectives of the Commonwealth of Independent States and Eurasia* (pp. 48–90). Hershey, PA: IGI Global. doi:10.4018/978-1-5225-3264-4.ch003

Durnalı, M., Orakcı, Ş., & Özkan, O. (2018). Turkey's Higher Education Potential for Human Capital of Eurasian Region. In O. Karnaukhova, A. Udovikina, & B. Christiansen (Eds.), *Economic and Geopolitical Perspectives of the Commonwealth of Independent States and Eurasia* (pp. 201–224). Hershey, PA: IGI Global. doi:10.4018/978-1-5225-3264-4.ch009

Elokhova, I. V., Dubrovskaya, J. V., & Kozonogova, E. V. (2018). Cross-Regional Interactions as a Source for Innovative Reformation: The Case of Russia. In D. Ushakov (Ed.), *Economic Reforms for Global Competitiveness* (pp. 141–161). Hershey, PA: IGI Global. doi:10.4018/978-1-5225-3856-1.ch008

Ermasova, N. B., & Ermasova, P. (2019). Public Capital Budgeting and Management Process in Russia. In A. Srithongrung, N. Ermasova, & J. Yusuf (Eds.), *Capital Management and Budgeting in the Public Sector* (pp. 113–133). Hershey, PA: IGI Global. doi:10.4018/978-1-5225-7329-6.ch006

Erokhin, V. (2015). Russia's Foreign Trade in Agricultural Commodities in Its Transition to Liberalization: A Path to Go Green. In A. Jean-Vasile, I. Andreea, & T. Adrian (Eds.), *Green Economic Structures in Modern Business and Society* (pp. 253–273). Hershey, PA: IGI Global. doi:10.4018/978-1-4666-8219-1.ch014

Erokhin, V. (2019). Arctic Connectivity for Sustainable Development: Major Actors, Policies, and Approaches. In V. Erokhin, T. Gao, & X. Zhang (Eds.), *Handbook of Research on International Collaboration, Economic Development, and Sustainability in the Arctic* (pp. 24–54). Hershey, PA: IGI Global. doi:10.4018/978-1-5225-6954-1.ch002

Fomicheva, E. V., & Shikun, M. S. (2018). Financial and Economic Security of BRICS Countries. In I. Nekrasova, O. Karnaukhova, & B. Christiansen (Eds.), *Fractal Approaches for Modeling Financial Assets and Predicting Crises* (pp. 139–150). Hershey, PA: IGI Global. doi:10.4018/978-1-5225-3767-0.ch008

Friedrich, P., & Chebotareva, M. (2017). Options for Applying Functional Overlapping Competing Jurisdictions (FOCJs) for Municipal Cooperation in Russia. In M. Lewandowski & B. Kożuch (Eds.), *Public Sector Entrepreneurship and the Integration of Innovative Business Models* (pp. 73–107). Hershey, PA: IGI Global. doi:10.4018/978-1-5225-2215-7.ch004

Gamidullaeva, L. A., Merkulova, N. S., Kryachkova, L. I., Kondratieva, Z. A., Efimova, Y. A., & Matukin, S. V. (2019). Emerging Trends and Opportunities for Industry Development at the Sub-National Level in Russia. In U. Benna (Ed.), *Industrial and Urban Growth Policies at the Sub-National, National, and Global Levels* (pp. 342–363). Hershey, PA: IGI Global. doi:10.4018/978-1-5225-7625-9.ch017

Gamidullaeva, L. A., Vasin, S. M., Shkarupeta, E. V., Tolstykh, T. O., Finogeev, A. G., Surovitskaya, G. V., & Kanarev, S. (2019). Emergence of Industry 4.0 Technologies: Leapfrogging Opportunity for the Russian Federation. In U. Benna (Ed.), *Industrial and Urban Growth Policies at the Sub-National, National, and Global Levels* (pp. 270–299). Hershey, PA: IGI Global. doi:10.4018/978-1-5225-7625-9.ch014

Horska, E., Moroz, S., & Galova, J. (2016). The EU – Ukraine – Russia Crisis Triangle: Evidence of Local and Global Consequences for International Trade. In V. Erokhin (Ed.), *Global Perspectives on Trade Integration and Economies in Transition* (pp. 105–125). Hershey, PA: IGI Global. doi:10.4018/978-1-5225-0451-1.ch006

Ilik, G. (2019). Restoring the Memory: The European Union as a Postnational Agent for Reconciliation of the Balkans. In V. Apryshchenko & O. Karnaukhova (Eds.), *Memory, Identity, and Nationalism in European Regions* (pp. 30–49). Hershey, PA: IGI Global. doi:10.4018/978-1-5225-8392-9.ch002

Ivolga, A., Trukhachev, A., & Elfimova, Y. (2019). Innovation-Driven Growth of Tourist Destinations in the Russian Arctic: Challenges to Sustainable Development. In V. Erokhin, T. Gao, & X. Zhang (Eds.), *Handbook of Research on International Collaboration, Economic Development, and Sustainability in the Arctic* (pp. 245–269). Hershey, PA: IGI Global. doi:10.4018/978-1-5225-6954-1.ch012

Karmaeva, N., & Kanonire, T. (2017). Institutional Legacy as a Context of the Implementation of International Rankings in the Russian Higher Education System. In K. Downing & F. Ganotice Jr., (Eds.), *World University Rankings and the Future of Higher Education* (pp. 368–392). Hershey, PA: IGI Global. doi:10.4018/978-1-5225-0819-9.ch019

Kaushal, V., & Sharma, S. (2017). Tourism Perspectives and Potential among BRIC Nations. In M. Dhiman (Ed.), *Opportunities and Challenges for Tourism and Hospitality in the BRIC Nations* (pp. 117–136). Hershey, PA: IGI Global. doi:10.4018/978-1-5225-0708-6.ch008

Keri, I., Gromova, E., & Sinelschikova, N. (2019). Features of Financial Policy Development by Russian Companies in Today's Conditions. In D. Ushakov (Ed.), *Global Trends of Modernization in Budgeting and Finance* (pp. 64–82). Hershey, PA: IGI Global. doi:10.4018/978-1-5225-7760-7.ch004

Khudzhatov, M. (2019). Non-Arctic Countries of Asia and Russia: Investment Collaboration in the High North. In V. Erokhin, T. Gao, & X. Zhang (Eds.), *Handbook of Research on International Collaboration, Economic Development, and Sustainability in the Arctic* (pp. 185–206). Hershey, PA: IGI Global. doi:10.4018/978-1-5225-6954-1.ch009

Kiregian, E. (2017). The Transformation of Russian Business Education and Its Outcomes: How Russia Moved Away from Marxism toward a Market Economy through Revitalized Business Education. In F. Topor (Ed.), *Handbook of Research on Individualism and Identity in the Globalized Digital Age* (pp. 457–477). Hershey, PA: IGI Global. doi:10.4018/978-1-5225-0522-8.ch020

Kojobekova, A. (2018). Are the Commonwealth of Independent States and Eurasian Union Able to Enhance Economic and Political Cooperation in the Post-Soviet Space? In O. Karnaukhova, A. Udovikina, & B. Christiansen (Eds.), *Economic and Geopolitical Perspectives of the Commonwealth of Independent States and Eurasia* (pp. 121–136). Hershey, PA: IGI Global. doi:10.4018/978-1-5225-3264-4.ch005

Kotlyarov, N. (2019). Russia-China Collaboration in the Arctic: Opportunities and Challenges. In V. Erokhin, T. Gao, & X. Zhang (Eds.), *Handbook of Research on International Collaboration, Economic Development, and Sustainability in the Arctic* (pp. 207–219). Hershey, PA: IGI Global. doi:10.4018/978-1-5225-6954-1.ch010

Kumar, A., & Legashova, A. (2017). An Analysis of Development of Domestic and Inbound Tourism in Russia. In M. Dhiman (Ed.), *Opportunities and Challenges for Tourism and Hospitality in the BRIC Nations* (pp. 252–264). Hershey, PA: IGI Global. doi:10.4018/978-1-5225-0708-6.ch016

Kuznetsov, M. Y., & Zhuplev, A. V. (2019). Russia: Traveling Scylla and Charybdis of Economic Nationalism – Could Economic Nationalism Be a Useful Tool to Boost Economic Growth and Development? In H. Chandan & B. Christiansen (Eds.), *International Firms' Economic Nationalism and Trade Policies in the Globalization Era* (pp. 74–98). Hershey, PA: IGI Global. doi:10.4018/978-1-5225-7561-0.ch005

Lagutina, M. (2018). The Eurasian Economic Union in the Context of Transformation of the International Trade System. In A. Özer (Ed.), *Globalization and Trade Integration in Developing Countries* (pp. 55–75). Hershey, PA: IGI Global. doi:10.4018/978-1-5225-4032-8.ch003

Lindström, N. B., & Cordeiro, C. M. (2018). Framing of National Image in a Climate of Socio-Political Uncertainty: A Study of IKEA and Volvo Car Corporation in Swedish and Russian News Media. In O. Karnaukhova, A. Udovikina, & B. Christiansen (Eds.), *Economic and Geopolitical Perspectives of the Commonwealth of Independent States and Eurasia* (pp. 137–156). Hershey, PA: IGI Global. doi:10.4018/978-1-5225-3264-4.ch006

Lipski, S., & Storozhenko, O. (2019). Russia's Circumpolar Territories Inhabited by Indigenous Peoples: Economic and Legal Aspects of Development. In V. Erokhin, T. Gao, & X. Zhang (Eds.), *Handbook of Research on International Collaboration, Economic Development, and Sustainability in the Arctic* (pp. 470–494). Hershey, PA: IGI Global. doi:10.4018/978-1-5225-6954-1.ch022

Mar Gálvez-Rodríguez, M. D., Saraite, L., Alonso-Cañadas, J., & Caba-Pérez, M. D. (2017). Stakeholder Engagement via Social Media in the Hospitality Sector: The Evidence from BRIC Countries. In M. Dhiman (Ed.), *Opportunities and Challenges for Tourism and Hospitality in the BRIC Nations* (pp. 15–30). Hershey, PA: IGI Global. doi:10.4018/978-1-5225-0708-6.ch002

Marchukov, A. (2019). Development of Slovak Public Diplomacy in the Post-Independence Period. In V. Apryshchenko & O. Karnaukhova (Eds.), *Memory, Identity, and Nationalism in European Regions* (pp. 78–97). Hershey, PA: IGI Global. doi:10.4018/978-1-5225-8392-9.ch004

Mohammed, K. (2018). What If the USSR Comes Back to Life Once Again?: Measuring CINC Index of Commonwealth of Independent States (CIS). In O. Karnaukhova, A. Udovikina, & B. Christiansen (Eds.), *Economic and Geopolitical Perspectives of the Commonwealth of Independent States and Eurasia* (pp. 252–268). Hershey, PA: IGI Global. doi:10.4018/978-1-5225-3264-4.ch011

Muminova, S., & Kopylov, Y. (2016). E-Design and E-Development of Real Estate Services in Russia. In V. Mkrttchian, A. Bershadsky, A. Bozhday, M. Kataev, & S. Kataev (Eds.), *Handbook of Research on Estimation and Control Techniques in E-Learning Systems* (pp. 486–499). Hershey, PA: IGI Global. doi:10.4018/978-1-4666-9489-7.ch034

Musaoğlu, N. (2018). “Sovereign Democracy” Discourse in the Russian Foreign Policy. In O. Karnaukhova, A. Udovikina, & B. Christiansen (Eds.), *Economic and Geopolitical Perspectives of the Commonwealth of Independent States and Eurasia* (pp. 178–200). Hershey, PA: IGI Global. doi:10.4018/978-1-5225-3264-4.ch008

Nadezhda, K., Elena, D., & Larisa, Z. (2019). Financial Behavior of Russian Population under Crisis Phenomena. In D. Ushakov (Ed.), *Global Trends of Modernization in Budgeting and Finance* (pp. 22–43). Hershey, PA: IGI Global. doi:10.4018/978-1-5225-7760-7.ch002

Orakcı, Ş., Durnalı, M., & Özkan, O. (2018). Curriculum Reforms in Turkey. In O. Karnaukhova, A. Udovikina, & B. Christiansen (Eds.), *Economic and Geopolitical Perspectives of the Commonwealth of Independent States and Eurasia* (pp. 225–251). Hershey, PA: IGI Global. doi:10.4018/978-1-5225-3264-4.ch010

Özer, A. C. (2018). An Analysis of Trade of the Eurasian Economic Union. In A. Özer (Ed.), *Globalization and Trade Integration in Developing Countries* (pp. 76–96). Hershey, PA: IGI Global. doi:10.4018/978-1-5225-4032-8.ch004

Petre, I. (2018). Study on the Evolution of the Meat Price Following the Russian Embargo. *International Journal of Sustainable Economies Management*, 7(2), 14–24. doi:10.4018/IJSEM.2018040102

Podolskaya, T. (2018). Alternative Financial Integration to Stimulate National Competitiveness: The Case of BRICS Countries. In D. Ushakov (Ed.), *Economic Reforms for Global Competitiveness* (pp. 162–179). Hershey, PA: IGI Global. doi:10.4018/978-1-5225-3856-1.ch009

Ponkin, I., Shevchenko, O., & Redkina, A. (2019). Legal, Ethical, and Integrity Issues in Sports Industry: The Russian Experience. In K. Margaritis (Ed.), *Law, Ethics, and Integrity in the Sports Industry* (pp. 169–201). Hershey, PA: IGI Global. doi:10.4018/978-1-5225-5387-8.ch009

Prabhakar, A. C. (2016). Trade and Economic Integration in BRICS: Towards Multi-Polarity. In V. Erokhin (Ed.), *Global Perspectives on Trade Integration and Economies in Transition* (pp. 45–57). Hershey, PA: IGI Global. doi:10.4018/978-1-5225-0451-1.ch003

Puffer, S. M., & McCarthy, D. J. (2018). History of the USSR and CIS. In O. Karnaukhova, A. Udovikina, & B. Christiansen (Eds.), *Economic and Geopolitical Perspectives of the Commonwealth of Independent States and Eurasia* (pp. 1–18). Hershey, PA: IGI Global. doi:10.4018/978-1-5225-3264-4.ch001

Rizk, E., & Zgheib, P. W. (2019). Financial Deficit in Lebanese Catholic Schools: Lack of Confidence and Declining Purchasing Power. In P. Zgheib (Ed.), *Impacts of Political Instability on Economics in the MENA Region* (pp. 199–214). Hershey, PA: IGI Global. doi:10.4018/978-1-5225-8247-2.ch008

Salman, D., & Bassim, M. A. (2019). Political Stability, Austerity Measures, External Imbalance, and Debt Impact on the Egyptian Economy. In P. Zgheib (Ed.), *Impacts of Political Instability on Economics in the MENA Region* (pp. 74–102). Hershey, PA: IGI Global. doi:10.4018/978-1-5225-8247-2.ch003

Samarina, V. P., Skufina, T. P., & Samarin, A. V. (2018). Regional Anti-Recessionary Reforms: Administrative Priorities and Economic Efficiency – The Case of the Russian Federation. In D. Ushakov (Ed.), *Economic Reforms for Global Competitiveness* (pp. 120–140). Hershey, PA: IGI Global. doi:10.4018/978-1-5225-3856-1.ch007

Sergunin, A. (2019). Russian Arctic Cities' Sustainable Development Strategies. In V. Erokhin, T. Gao, & X. Zhang (Eds.), *Handbook of Research on International Collaboration, Economic Development, and Sustainability in the Arctic* (pp. 495–511). Hershey, PA: IGI Global. doi:10.4018/978-1-5225-6954-1.ch023

Shahzad, F. (2019). An Analysis of Internationalization Theories and Behavior of Finnish Retail SMEs in Russia. In N. Teixeira, T. Costa, & I. Lisboa (Eds.), *Handbook of Research on Entrepreneurship, Innovation, and Internationalization* (pp. 490–520). Hershey, PA: IGI Global. doi:10.4018/978-1-5225-8479-7.ch019

Shevchenko, D., & Arku, H. K. (2019). State Institutions of Financial Support for Small Business in Volatile Economies: Possible Application of Russian Experience in Ghana. In J. Carvalho & E. Sabino (Eds.), *Strategy and Superior Performance of Micro and Small Businesses in Volatile Economies* (pp. 1–17). Hershey, PA: IGI Global. doi:10.4018/978-1-5225-7888-8.ch001

Smirnova, O., Korovkin, V., & Plaksenkov, E. (2018). Inclusive Disruption: The Role of Financial Technologies in Filling Financial Inclusion Gaps in Russia. In A. Zhuplev (Ed.), *Disruptive Technologies for Business Development and Strategic Advantage* (pp. 153–186). Hershey, PA: IGI Global. doi:10.4018/978-1-5225-4148-6.ch005

Smith, N., & Thomas, E. (2016). Exploring the Social Impact of Foreign Direct Investment on Institutional Change: The Case of Russia. In M. Khan (Ed.), *Multinational Enterprise Management Strategies in Developing Countries* (pp. 198–214). Hershey, PA: IGI Global. doi:10.4018/978-1-5225-0276-0.ch010

Smith, N., & Thomas, E. (2016). On the Relationship between Informal and Formal Institutions, Foreign Direct Investment, and Innovation in Emerging Markets: The Case of Russia, India, and China, 1990-2014. In M. Khan (Ed.), *Multinational Enterprise Management Strategies in Developing Countries* (pp. 176–197). Hershey, PA: IGI Global. doi:10.4018/978-1-5225-0276-0.ch009

Tanrısever, O. F., & Türkmen, H. S. (2018). The Securitization Theory and Migration: The Case of Russia's Securitization of Europe's Migration Crisis. In Ş. Erçetin (Ed.), *Social Considerations of Migration Movements and Immigration Policies* (pp. 1–12). Hershey, PA: IGI Global. doi:10.4018/978-1-5225-3322-1.ch001

Teper, Y. (2017). How Civic is Russia's New Civil Religion and How Religious is the Church? In E. Lewin, E. Bick, & D. Naor (Eds.), *Comparative Perspectives on Civil Religion, Nationalism, and Political Influence* (pp. 125–155). Hershey, PA: IGI Global. doi:10.4018/978-1-5225-0516-7.ch005

Tianming, G. (2018). Food Security and Rural Development on Emerging Markets of Northeast Asia: Cases of Chinese North and Russian Far East. In V. Erokhin (Ed.), *Establishing Food Security and Alternatives to International Trade in Emerging Economies* (pp. 155–176). Hershey, PA: IGI Global. doi:10.4018/978-1-5225-2733-6.ch008

Tokbaeva, D. (2019). Media Entrepreneurs and Market Dynamics: Case of Russian Media Markets. *Journal of Media Management and Entrepreneurship*, *1*(1), 40–56. doi:10.4018/JMME.2019010103

Tsygankov, S., & Gasanova, E. (2017). Electronification of the Public Procurement System: A Comparative Analysis of the Experience of the Russian Federation and Ukraine. In R. Shakya (Ed.), *Digital Governance and E-Government Principles Applied to Public Procurement* (pp. 267–277). Hershey, PA: IGI Global. doi:10.4018/978-1-5225-2203-4.ch013

Ushakov, D., & Rubinskaya, E. (2018). Reforming of the State Immigration Policy in the Context of Globalization: On the Example of Russia. In D. Ushakov (Ed.), *Economic Reforms for Global Competitiveness* (pp. 230–248). Hershey, PA: IGI Global. doi:10.4018/978-1-5225-3856-1.ch012

Voronenko, A., Tomilov, M., & Greizik, S. (2019). Collaboration Between Russia and the Countries of Northeast Asia in the Arctic. In V. Erokhin, T. Gao, & X. Zhang (Eds.), *Handbook of Research on International Collaboration, Economic Development, and Sustainability in the Arctic* (pp. 162–184). Hershey, PA: IGI Global. doi:10.4018/978-1-5225-6954-1.ch008

Windsor, D. (2018). Corruption in the CIS and Eurasia: Sources, Consequences, and Possible Solutions. In O. Karnaukhova, A. Udovikina, & B. Christiansen (Eds.), *Economic and Geopolitical Perspectives of the Commonwealth of Independent States and Eurasia* (pp. 91–120). Hershey, PA: IGI Global. doi:10.4018/978-1-5225-3264-4.ch004

Yablonsky, S. (2016). E-Finance Services in Russia. In I. Lee (Ed.), *Encyclopedia of E-Commerce Development, Implementation, and Management* (pp. 1215–1228). Hershey, PA: IGI Global. doi:10.4018/978-1-4666-9787-4.ch087

Zgheib, P. W. (2019). Transnational Protocol Authority for Economic Gains in Water Management. In P. Zgheib (Ed.), *Impacts of Political Instability on Economics in the MENA Region* (pp. 1–27). Hershey, PA: IGI Global. doi:10.4018/978-1-5225-8247-2.ch001

Zhuplev, A., & Kuznetsov, M. (2017). The Role of Inward FDI for Economic Growth at the Time of Downturn: The Case of Russia. In T. Dorożyński & A. Kuna-Marszałek (Eds.), *Outward Foreign Direct Investment (FDI) in Emerging Market Economies* (pp. 161–199). Hershey, PA: IGI Global. doi:10.4018/978-1-5225-2345-1.ch009

Zhuplev, A., & Shtykhno, D. A. (2015). Energy and Sustainability in the European Region: The Russian Factor. In K. Thomas (Ed.), *Handbook of Research on Sustainable Development and Economics* (pp. 118–158). Hershey, PA: IGI Global. doi:10.4018/978-1-4666-8433-1.ch007

About the Authors

Bogdan Anatolyevich Ershov was born on June 18, 1982 in the city of Voronezh (Russian Federation). In 1999 he entered the Voronezh State Pedagogical University as a full-time department of the Faculty of History, which he graduated in 2004 with a degree in history with an additional specialty in social pedagogy. In 2007 he defended his thesis on the theme: "The Church of the Russian province in the XIX century (on the materials of the Voronezh province)" in the specialty 07.00.02 - the history of Russia. In 2012 he defended his doctoral thesis on the topic "The Russian Orthodox Church in the System of State Relations in the 19th - Early 20th Centuries (Based on Materials From the Central Black Earth Provinces)" in the specialty Domestic History. In 2013 he was awarded the academic title of associate professor. From 2014 to the present, Bogdan Yershov is a professor at the Department of Philosophy, Sociology and History of the Voronezh State Technical University.

Mukhina Natalya Evgenievna was born on February 5, 1982, in Voronezh. In 1988, she entered secondary school No. 92. In 1997 she moved to school # 23 in a secondary school and later received an additional certificate in the specialty "Lawyer" with conferring the qualification "Junior Lawyer". In 1999 she graduated from school. In the same year she entered the Voronezh State Pedagogical University, after which in 2004 she was awarded a qualification - a history teacher with a degree in History. From 2004 to 2007 she was trained in full-time graduate school of the Voronezh State Technical University with a degree in Domestic History. In 2007, after completing postgraduate studies, she successfully defended her thesis. From 2001 to 2004 she worked as a tutor in the Municipal Educational Institution of the Pro-Minas No.3. From 2006 to 2007 she worked as an assistant at the Department of History and Political Science at the Voronezh State Technical University. From 2007 to 2018 in the Voronezh State Technical University at the Department of History and Political Science worked first as a senior lecturer, and then worked as an associate professor. From 2018 to the present, he has been working at the department of "Humanitarian and socio-economic disciplines" of the Federal State Official Military Educational Institution of Higher Education "Military Educational and Scientific Centre of the Air Force N.E. Zhukovsky and Y.A. Gagarin Air Force Academy" (Voronezh) the Ministry of Defence of the Russian Federation.

Igor Ashmarov was born on November 18, 1975. In 1997, he graduated from the history department of the Voronezh State University. In 2003 Ashmarov I.A. defended his thesis. Thesis: "Economic institutions of the labor market" (place of defense - Voronezh State University). In 2009, he was awarded the academic title of associate professor. From 2014 to the present, Ashmarov Igor has been working as an assistant professor in the department of humanitarian and socio-economic disciplines of the Voronezh State Institute of Arts.

Index

www.ingramcontent.com/pod-product-compliance
Lightning Source LLC
LaVergne TN
LVHW061533290926
849162LV00004B/779